SEAMAN SCHMUCATELLI

OPS BOXES WILL BE NAMED AFTER
1980S HAIR METAL BANDS INSTEA
OF POKÉMON CHARACTERS.

PIKACHU:

Okay. But Nickelback?

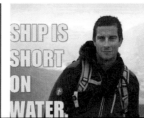

WHAT'S YOUR CALL SIGN?

WHAT'S YOUR CALL SIGN?

THE HILARIOUS STORIES BEHIND

W T F

A NAVAL AVIATION TRADITION

BEN "LOBO" TAGGART

SCHIFFER MILITARY

4880 Lower Valley Road   Atglen, PA 19310

TO | **ADRIENNE TAGGART,**
Amazing woman and wonderful mother.

Dark skies loom over an MV-22B as it lifts from the deck of USS *Wasp* somewhere on the South China Sea. Shhhh! Don't tell the People's Republic of China!

Other Schiffer books on related subjects
Vulture's Row: Thirty Years in Naval Aviation, Paul T. Gillcrist,
  ISBN 978-0-7643-0047-9
*TOPGUN: The Legacy; The Complete History of TOPGUN
  and Its Impact on Tactical Aviation,* Brad Elward,
  ISBN 978-0-7643-6254-5

Designed by Justin Watkinson
Type set in Industry/Minion Pro

ISBN: 978-0-7643-6638-3
Printed in China

Published by Schiffer Publishing, Ltd.
4880 Lower Valley Road
Atglen, PA 19310
Phone: (610) 593-1777; Fax: (610) 593-2002
Email: Info@schifferbooks.com
Web: www.schifferbooks.com

For our complete selection of fine books on this and related subjects, please visit our website at www.schifferbooks.com. You may also write for a free catalog.

Schiffer Publishing's titles are available at special discounts for bulk purchases for sales promotions or premiums. Special editions, including personalized covers, corporate imprints, and excerpts, can be created in large quantities for special needs. For more information, contact the publisher.

We are always looking for people to write books on new and related subjects. If you have an idea for a book, please contact us at proposals@schifferbooks.com.

CONTENTS

An F-35B comes hovering in for a landing. Get out the way!

An F-35B pilot conducts his preflight checks. He's about to get some of the pinkie time.

PREFACE

PREFACE

I would like to state for the record that I started writing this book long before I knew that *Top Gun: Maverick* was a thing. So before you accuse me with your wee beady accusing eyes, just know that this is not me jumping on the bandwagon as renewed interest in naval aviation takes hold thanks to Pete Mitchell, call sign Maverick. If I make a little coin off this book thanks to the efforts of Tom Cruise, I will be only too happy to do so. However, I didn't write this book for the purpose of exploiting the attention naval aviation may have received as a result of the next installment of a movie that ushered in the "Golden Era of Naval Aviation" (1986–1991).

My idea for writing this book came from my time in Kabul, Afghanistan, of all places. I was way outside the cockpit by then, working as an advisor to the chief of the Afghan border police. The advisor team I was on had a lot of Brits. One day over lunch I was sharing call sign stories with my British friends, which they seemed to genuinely find humorous. It occurred to me that if these stories were funny to people who didn't have the foggiest notion of what or who naval aviators were, it might be funny to other people too. One of the limeys recommended that I write a book of collected call signs, and a seed was planted in my little brain. Little did I know that my next assignment would give me a golden opportunity to collect call sign stories. I was assigned as the air operations officer on USS *Wasp* and later USS *America*. These ships are like mini aircraft carriers, and both carry a composite squadron of Marine MV-22Bs, CH-53Es, and F-35Bs. In addition there is a search-and-rescue (SAR) detachment (det) of Navy MH-60Ss on board. I had access to a slew of pilots and naval flight officers (NFOs) from multiple aircraft communities, both in the Navy and Marine Corps. What better environment to collect call sign stories?

You might be wondering what a call sign is exactly. For the purposes of this book, a call sign is really just a nickname. Some guys will use individual call signs to address a specific person in a flight (I'm told that Tac Air guys still use individual call signs this way as a matter of standard operating procedure). It should be noted that there are different kinds of call signs. Any station on a radio in the military has a call sign, whether it's a tank, troops on the ground, or a ship. The call sign an aircrew may use while flying could be something like Trash One-Two or Knightrider Zero-One. This is not the same as the nicknames we use to refer to each other in day-to-day situations. In squadron spaces, wardrooms, ready rooms, ship's passageways, and bars in exotic foreign lands, or in emails about the most-mundane work details, call signs are used as familial monikers among professionals in naval aviation. Each time a call sign is uttered, there is a touch of familial love that signifies the common experience all naval aviators have shared, from the hallowed halls of Aviation Preflight Indoctrination (API) at Naval Air Station Pensacola to flying in the fleet as a no-kidding, death-cheating naval aviator or naval flight officer. And in that familial touch is the slight nostalgic remembrance of the naval aviators and NFOs who came before we did, who flew off straight flight decks made of wood, shot down MiGs over North Korea, landed on hilltops in the DMZ to resupply beleaguered Marines, languished in the Hanoi Hilton, sundowned the Tomcat, or dropped bombs on insurgents over Fallujah. This book is an attempt to preserve a piece of naval aviation history that, right or wrong, is dying a slow, painful death. I feel it's worth remembering, and I strongly believe that someone has to preserve these stories before they all fade into history with the naval aviators and NFOs who lived them.

Toward the end of my last patrol on USS *America*, I was acutely aware that I was about to witness the last great fly-off of my twenty-seven years as a marine. The reinforced Marine Corps MV-22B squadron was leaving the ship to return to their home station on Okinawa. I was already feeling nostalgic for the last two years I had spent on USS *Wasp* and USS *America*, where I was privileged to watch flight operations up close and in person. It was my job to plan how the six spots and the tram line were used by the embarked squadrons, and I could never get over how amazing and beautiful it was to witness aircraft "bounce" on and off the ship.

"All of this has happened before . . ." is the famous opening line to J. M. Barrie's *Peter Pan*, a story about a strange dreamlike adventure to a land that never was. Being thousands of miles from home, off on adventures while the majority of my fellow Americans slept soundly in their beds, reminded me of Neverland, and the people I worked with always reminded me of the "Lost Boys." Most people have no idea of the shenanigans we get ourselves into in naval aviation, gallivanting around the globe, flying sexy aircraft, hitting strange and exotic liberty ports, and living a life of danger and adventure, all in the daily routine course of defending our nation's maritime interests. We are really just a bunch of lost boys and girls who play war with Aborigines and fight pirates. "And it will all happen again."

Look, I saw it all during my time in the Marines flying CH-46s and C-12s, or enviously watching other people fly gull gray aircraft from the ship; the night flights in green-tinted splendor on night vision goggles, the rough days at sea or getting shot at by "celebratory" fire over Iraq, the liberty ports in exotic locations, all the bad decisions, the camaraderie and adventure, all of it—I saw it all! It was all so incredibly cool. You try walking around in a flight suit, wings upon your chest. You try walking away from an aircraft you just landed, somehow avoiding the "inscrutable immutable" and living to fly another day. Go ahead, try it, and tell me it doesn't get in your head. Tell me wearing a green onesie to work every day doesn't make you feel cool, doesn't make you look at other people like, "Why aren't you cool too?" Go ahead, tell me it doesn't make you feel like you're special! I dare you! It's a thing, and our wingless comrades who wear blue coveralls or green digi cammies know this about us. They hate us for it, even if they like us on an individual basis. And on top of it all, we give each other cute little nicknames, like we're in the Mickey Mouse Club.

The ground pounders and SHOEs can maybe take some comfort in knowing that we don't really like our call signs. They're hurtful and mean spirited, given to us by our fellow flight-suit-wearing comrades to make fun of something we're sensitive about, to make light of something so embarrassing that we lie to our parents about what our call signs really mean. However, the secret about our call signs is something so beautiful that it defies logic and reason. Call signs are not what they appear to be on the surface. They're something much more, and luckily for you, you have this book to read. You get to find out all about it if you choose to read on. I hope you will, and I hope the next time you see a naval aviator or naval flight officer that this book inspires you to ask them one question: "Hey! What's your call sign?"

Major Ben "Lobo" Taggart
November 2022

✪ DJ LOBO

FOD (foreign-object debris) walk is a special time of day on a flight deck–equipped ship. A ship's crew and the embarked squadron personnel stand shoulder to shoulder and walk from stem to stern with their heads down and on a swivel in search of tiny bits of debris that can get sucked into a jet engine, causing millions of dollars in damage. One of my collateral duties was providing music for the FOD walkers. Using my iPhone, a rubber band, a JBL speaker in a cardboard box, and a hand mic connected to the flight deck loudspeaker, I played an eclectic mix of tunes for all the music fans out on FOD walk. A book's foreword is sort of the FOD walk of any book. So in honor of the flight operations that you're about to undertake while reading this book, here is an example of a normal announcement at the beginning of FOD walk on the ship. It went something like this: "Good morning, my fellow Americans! It's another fabulous day on USS *America*, much like yesterday and the day before and the day before that! It's time for the FOD walk radio show! I'm your host, DJ Lobo, live on the mic from flight deck control on KUSA, the Pacific Fleet's number one imaginary radio station! Just a quick reminder to keep your head on a swivel and keep hydrated out there. This next jam is going out to the Grapes for doing that groovy thing you do!"

A NOTE ABOUT THE PHOTOGRAPHY:

All the photos that appear in this book were taken between the summer of 2018 and the summer of 2020 on board USS *Wasp* and USS *America*. The photos are a depiction of flight operations aboard these two ships and, as such, depict the people and the aircraft that operate in the incredibly demanding and unforgiving environment of a large flight deck on a US Navy ship. Juxtaposed against the funny stories behind naval aviation call signs, my hope is that through these photos the reader will gain an appreciation for the amazing work performed everyday by flight deck crews, aircrew, and all of the personnel who contribute to this incredible profession of arms. The images in this book are limited to flight operations on board "amphib" ships specifically designed to support Marine expeditionary units, and therefore the photography of aircraft is a bit Marine Corps centric. As such, it was my hope that I could tell the story of naval aviation as I saw it during my two-year tour as the Marine Corps' Japan-based air operations officer on *Wasp* and *America*. While the call signs presented in this book represent all of naval aviation, the photos do not.

Get out of your racks, get out of your shops, get out of your holes! Come on up to the flight deck for another glorious FOD walk-down.

CHAPTER 1

Before I go on and on, let me clear something up. There is a doctrinal distinction between naval flight officers (NFO) and naval aviators (pilots). The main difference between pilots and NFOs is that pilots wiggle the sticks and NFOs don't. When the pilot pulls back on the stick, the houses get smaller, and when they push forward on the stick, the houses get bigger. NFOs generally don't wiggle the sticks. They operate all the varied weapons, sensors, and communications systems on aircraft that are either too complex for a pilot to handle all by him- or herself or that require a multicrew effort. For instance, the P-3 Orion, originally designed to hunt submarines and kill them, has all kinds of gizmos and gadgets in the back that are operated by NFOs, who may never see the cockpit.

Pilots like to believe there is an NFO inferiority complex. Officially, NFO is an initialism for naval flight officer. Snickering pilots call NFOs "nonflying officers" because they don't wiggle the sticks. There's a little bit of a one-sided rivalry between pilots and NFOs. According to pilots, NFOs wanted to be pilots but their eyesight sucked, so they had to settle for the next best thing. Pilots might tell a new NFO to "strap in, sit on your hands, and tell me how smooth my landing was." Essentially, pilots can sometimes be douchebags to NFOs, who supposedly have a collective inferiority complex to douchebag pilots. (Please remember this book is being written by a pilot.) In truth, there are a million rivalries in the military, and most of them are all in good fun. Pilots and NFOs get along just fine, sort of like Maverick and Goose.

Half airplane, half helicopter, half ass at both, the MV-22B Osprey comes in to land on board USS *Wasp* somewhere on the Sea of Japan.

Huddled against the wind, Marine Corps F-35B plane captains wait for their pilots.

There's a joke about NFOs that goes something like this: Two student NFOs at flight school were studying in the ready room in preparation for their training flights the next day. They were the very best of friends. BFF doesn't come close to describing how close they were. Another fellow student NFO entered the ready room wearing the gold wings of a pilot. The two pals studying in the ready room asked why he was wearing pilot wings. Their former friend and colleague smugly told them to go upstairs and find out for themselves. Then he flipped them off and sauntered out of the room. So the two best pals ran upstairs to discover a vending machine that sold pilot wings for a buck fifty. They could finally shuffle off the shame of NFOdom and be real pilots! Pal number one had two dollars and pal number two had a only dollar (I promise this isn't Common Core math). Pal number one said, "I'll get my wings, and when my change comes out I'll give it to you so you can get yours." So the first guy inserted his two dollars into the machine, grabbed his new wings from the tray, and pocketed his change. Then he pinned his new wings on his chest and sauntered off without a word to his best pal. His pal, aghast, said, "Hey, I thought you were gonna give me your change?" The newly minted pilot said, "Get lost, NFO; get your own fifty cents." You can be the judge as to whether or not this joke says more about pilots than it does NFOs.

Now that I've sorted out the differences between naval aviators and naval flight officers, let me tell you a little something about these fine American sky devils. Pilots and NFOs are graduates of one of the US Navy's flight schools (jet, helicopter, maritime patrol, cargo, NFO, etc.) and, in some cases, graduates of the US Air Force's primary flight school (there's an exchange program between the Navy and Air Force, where the Air Force trains a few jarheads and squids to fly, and the Navy and Marines teach some airedales to fly). Once winged, they've gone on to one of the fleet replacement squadrons to learn how to fly and operate in "their" aircraft, whichever one that will be within the Naval Services' inventory. They have endured all kinds of monsters for instructor pilots (IPs), and they've been hazed within the legal bounds of the US Department of Defense's hazing policy at the fleet replacement squadron (FRS) and in their fleet squadrons (zero tolerance? yeah, right!). They've received some of the finest flight and tactical training in the world, and they've worked in the fleet to execute and operate at the highest levels of professionalism and proficiency. They have also consumed ungodly amounts of alcohol at squadron parties, wetting-downs, hail and farewells (hail and bails), nights out on liberty, kangaroo courts, and backyard BBQs in base housing or at the bachelor officers quarters (BOQ).

They've become experts at operating their aircraft in austere and unforgiving environments. Naval aviators and NFOs are better than everyone else because they have had it drilled into their heads that they are the best of the best. It's the lie that becomes true, a self-fulfilling prophecy like no other. For the most part, they're nonconformist, type A alphas, who tend to follow rules written in blood, and break them at their own peril. In the incredibly unforgiving environment of operating aircraft on and off of naval shipping, pilots and NFOs are fiercely intolerant of those in their ranks who don't learn this profession as though their lives depended on their professional proficiency and skill . . . because their lives sure as hell depend on their professional proficiency and skill.

The bible for pilots and NFOs is the Naval Aviation Training and Standardization Operations and Procedures (NATOPS) manual. What a mouthful! It's really more like the Bible, the Koran, and the Talmud all rolled into one. Every word in the NATOPS is written in blood. Flat-hatting in aircraft is prohibited because more pilots have died "buzzing the tower" than there are admirals' daughters! That's written in blood. Conducting aerobatics in the CH-53E is prohibited. Why? Because someone attempted an unbriefed barrel roll in one and crashed, killing all on board. That's written in blood. Each aircraft and each ship that has a flight deck has its very own NATOPS. Every naval aviator and NFO better damn sure understand what the NATOPS allows and what it prohibits. Every note, warning, and caution exists because someone somewhere learned the hard way.

Practitioners of naval aviation are professional perfectionists, smooth, calm under extreme pressure, nervous, overstressed, overthinking, and way overpaid to do something so incredibly thrilling ("I can't believe I'm getting paid for this" is a common sentiment uttered while flying, although never said on the ground). Your standard pilot or NFO is an adventurous thrill seeker, a calculated risk taker, a geek at heart, sincere and unwavering, and a hell of a lot of fun to party with. They see obstacles only as something to go through, over, or around, or to disregard completely; an obstacle is merely a formality. Mission is everything. They carry with them an undying bias for action. Pilots and NFOs are an intense breed, who can switch from cool and relaxed, jovial and welcoming, to steely-eyed life-takers at the drop of a hat. They're some of the nicest people you will ever meet, who also happen to be some of the deadliest killers the planet has ever known. They love each other, and they love this profession. You can't do this job without being permanently changed by it. Once a naval aviator or naval flight officer, always a naval aviator or naval flight officer. You better believe it!

So of course, the naval aviation sense of humor is sophomoric and idiotic. It's hard to explain why, other than the overly simplistic explanation that somehow the pressures of the job and the risk to life and limb require a certain kind of levity. We turn to levity to relieve the pressure, because regardless of the risk, we adore this profession. Humor helps us accept the risk and the mounds of BS we have to wade through in order to "kick the tires and light the fires." Ultimately, anyone who wants to do this job has to learn to laugh in the faces of danger and death, because you'd never strap in if you didn't. That's not a brag, that's science. We'd go nuts if we didn't laugh at ourselves and at each other. Everyone gets teased and made fun of, and there is very little sensitivity to whatever it is that someone might take great offense to or be incredibly self-conscious about. As such, naval aviation call signs are a unique blend of mean-spirited teasing, familial love, and camaraderie that somehow defies an all-encompassing explanation.

I think the first thing that comes to mind when non-naval aviation folks think about call signs is the original motion picture on the subject, *Top Gun*. There were really only two believable call signs in that movie, "Goose" and "Merlin," both of whom were radar intercept officers (RIO). RIO is what NFOs were called in the F-14 because the entire aircraft was built around the Phoenix missile, which used radar to track and kill enemy planes from over 100 miles away. All the pilots in *Top Gun* had cool call signs such as "Viper," "Ice-man," and of course "Maverick." The technical advisors for that movie failed to tell the director the truth about call signs: call signs are never flattering. You could be the ace of the base, the best thing to ever happen to naval aviation, the cream of the crop! It doesn't matter; your fellow naval aviators will still find a way to knock some of that chip off your shoulder. One way to do that is to give you a nickname that you will hate.

Take as an example the late John Glenn. He was the first man to orbit the earth, and an ace Marine fighter pilot in World War II and Korea. He had a distinguished career as a US senator, and in retirement he was the oldest man ever to go into space. That's one hell of a career for a naval aviator. His call sign was Magnet Ass. During the Korean War, his strafing runs against Communist targets were just a little too low. Far too often he would return to base with holes in the bottom of his airplane from the shrapnel that was created when his North Korean and Chinese targets would explode directly underneath him. Sounds like he really gave it to the enemy and was committed to killing his target, right? Well, yes, but no. There were plenty of good pilots, brave and true, who managed to return to base without shrapnel from their own ammunition in the bottom of their planes, while still destroying enemy targets at rates equal to or greater than our hero. The airframes guys in Glenn's squadron didn't much care for all of the extra work he provided them. The maintenance officer didn't much care for having another airplane that was out of the fight for a while, nor did he much appreciate the ire he would get from the operations officer constantly on his butt about up-and-ready airplanes available for mission tasking, you know, in the middle of a war:

An MH-60S Seahawk lifts from the deck at the beginning of flight ops, headed to the Starboard Delta for hours of turns, waiting for the worst to happen.

Ops officer: "Hey, is jet 12 up and ready for tasking?"
Maintenance officer: "Nope!"
Ops officer: "Why not?! There's a war on!"
Maintenance officer: "Guess who flew it last?"
Ops officer: "Magnet Ass. That son of a . . . !"

Magnet Ass was not given as a compliment.

Senator John McCain, another notable naval aviator turned politician, had a fairly notorious military career. He was a long-term guest at the Hanoi Hilton, where he courageously refused special treatment offered to him when the North Vietnamese discovered that his father was the commander of the US Pacific Fleet. Before he was shot down over Hanoi, McCain had crashed four aircraft due to pilot error and had survived the USS *Forrestal* fire, after an electrical malfunction on a nearby F-4 Phantom caused a Zuni rocket to fire across the flight deck and slam into the external fuel tank of the A-4 Skyhawk McCain was sitting in. But before any of that, John McCain caroused, partied, and drank like a frat boy who didn't know he wasn't in college anymore. Notably, he had once dated an exotic dancer named Marie while he was at flight school in Pensacola, who was known as "the Flame of Florida." His call sign was Playboy because of his rowdy and raucous lifestyle, and for his particular penchant for easy women.

There's always something. You could do something stupid and embarrassing while on liberty in Thailand, or your last name rhymes with penis, or you're as ugly as a Kardashian meltdown. That's how it is. There's no escaping it. However, before you read this book and think to yourself that we're a bunch of cotton-headed ninny-muggins, consider the beauty and brilliance of why we call each other such terrible and disgusting names. If there is one thing I want you, the dear reader, to take away from this book, it's this: call signs are meant to take something that someone is insecure about or embarrassed by and turn it into a nickname that becomes a term of endearment, a badge of honor, a moniker that says, "You're one of us." More than anything else, call signs are about camaraderie and belonging. Try not to forget that when you read about LAMCHOP and FUNGUS.

Some naval aviators and NFOs come to like their call signs, but they won't ever let that be known. You can't have someone out there who likes their call sign. I think it actually says something to that effect in the NATOPS. This book has been a challenge to write. Many call signs, especially these days, are not very funny. My call sign is "Lobo," which I like to tell people means lone wolf in Spanish, because I'm an alpha hunter and killer. It doesn't. Lobo is short for "Lost Boy." I was given that call sign because when I showed up to my first squadron straight out of the FRS, I was "lost in the sauce"; lost like a kid who ends up somewhere they're not supposed to be. I had been an enlisted Marine in a previous life, and I didn't quite know how to behave like an officer. It was funny to the guys in my squadron at the time, but not funny enough for this book—other than the fact that it's written here to help explain why not all call signs made the cut. I asked every pilot and NFO I met during my two years on *Wasp* and *America* what their call sign was, and 85 percent of the time I was left disappointed. Many of the stories were just boring. Luckily for me, most aviators know someone who has a good call sign story. Most of the stories in this book I received secondhand and by word of mouth. I wrote most of them down on napkins in the wardroom while my friends told me about this one dude in their first squadron who . . . well, you'll see.

Naval aviators and NFOs are excellent storytellers, and this is kind of a pastime for those of us privileged enough to wear wings of gold—sitting around telling funny stories from flying days gone by. After a while you sort of collect stories that you retell over and over again whenever pilots and NFOs sit around telling stories. It occurred to me that if these stories were not recorded, they would be lost forever with the pilots and NFOs who earned them. Some may have been passed down for a

couple of years as an oral record, but most would have been lost. In fact, most have been lost. There are thousands of men and women who have worn the gold wings of naval aviators and naval flight officers, and their call sign stories, for the most part, are lost to history.

⊜★⊜ LEVITY IS THE BEST MEDICINE

Naval aviation in particular is very unforgiving. The slightest error made by a pilot or maintainer can lead to a catastrophic failure of an essential system and ultimately end in a crash. People die doing this job far too regularly, and the loss of aircrew is devastating to the naval aviation community, the families, and squadron mates. Two CH-46Es were conducting aerial-gunnery training in the Kuwaiti desert when one of the lead aircraft's engines suddenly and completely disintegrated, which then caused catastrophic damage to the remaining engine.

A fireball swept through the cabin, causing flash burns to the crewmen in the back and to the arms and necks of the pilots up front. With the fireball came smoke, which completely obscured both pilots' vision. The dash-two aircraft watched in horror as the mortally damaged aircraft rolled over and barreled toward the ground. They were only 800 feet above the desert when the engine blew, so there wasn't much time to recover from the unusual attitude. The flying pilot's immediate response was to pull back on the stick and drop the collective. By some miracle this righted the aircraft, and it entered into a very sloppy autorotation. The aircraft smacked into the ground, but all on board survived the initial impact.

Unfortunately for one crewman, who was standing in the crew doorway, one of the rotor blades smashed through the tunnel and ripped him in two. The other crew chief, badly burned as a second wall of fire swept through the aircraft, stayed low and crawled his way to the crew door. Once the aircraft came to rest, he made for the exit. The two pilots, assuming that both crewmen were dead, leapt from their seats and together ran for a ditch 100 feet to the right side of the aircraft. The fire in the aircraft was raging, and the ammunition was beginning to cook off, sending rounds in every direction. Just as the remaining crew chief reached the door, another explosion ripped through the cabin and, by the grace of God, blew the crew chief clear. With second- and third-degree burns covering most of his body, and mostly naked except for his flight helmet, gloves, and boots, the crew chief landed in the ditch next to his pilots.

Sensing the danger of the ammunition cooking off, the aircraft commander asked the crew chief if he could run, and he said that he could. They all took off running as fast as their feet could carry them. The dash-two aircraft, who had witnessed the entire event, landed to retrieve the downed crew and flew them back to the ship for emergency medical treatment. The story is tragic, no doubt. A Marine crew chief lost his life on this day. But sometimes the gallows humor of aircrew can be the exact thing needed to ease the tension of an extreme situation such as the one described above.

The surviving crew chief was best friends with one of the other crew chiefs in the squadron, and together they were maniacal fans of the TV cartoon *The Simpsons*. They could hold entire conversations just using quotes from their favorite cartoon. In one favorite episode, a daredevil attempts to jump a local canyon on his motorcycle. For added danger, the river below is filled with alligators, and the shores of the river are covered in broken glass and rusty barbed wire. The daredevil jumps his motorcycle and lands in the center of the waiting crocodiles. He was then dragged through the broken glass and barbed wire to his rescue and eventually to a waiting ambulance. As the daredevil is taken away on the stretcher, the news crews begin asking him questions about the failed jump. Broken, bruised, and battered, the daredevil suddenly sits up on the stretcher, flashes his famous smile, and gives his adoring fans a thumbs-up before being whisked away to a hospital.

You're used to seeing the big-deck aircraft carriers. The flight ops depicted in this book all took place from one of these bad boys. Known in the amphib Navy as gators, LHD/LHA amphib ships are designed to support Marines during amphibious operations in war and peace.

Back to our story. By the time the remaining helicopter in the section returned to the ship, everyone was aware of the mishap. When the crew chief, burned and broken, was removed from the aircraft and taken to triage on a stretcher, his best friend looked on in shocked silence. The injured crew chief, seeing his friend's face and worried that his friend might take this hard, immediately sat up on the stretcher, flashed his familiar grin, and gave his best friend a thumbs-up. The injured crew chief's best friend immediately broke into laughter. The joke was more important than the injuries. In case you're wondering, the bruised and battered crew chief in our story eventually returned to flying after a long recovery.

Many of the stories may seem appalling, crude, and offensive to some. For someone who has never been in the military, much of our behavior may seem a bit inappropriate, even immature (the horror, the horror!). As evidence of the kind of humor that makes the cut among the "best of the best," I give you "Sky Penis." You may recall a news story in which the crew of an F/A-18G Growler drew a massive penis in the sky over western Washington with their contrail. The two Navy lieutenants faced severe reprimands from the brass for embarrassing the Navy. As immature as it was for these two clowns to draw a penis in the sky, using a multimillion-dollar jet aircraft, you can't help but admire their flying skill. I bet even the brass was secretly impressed, while Russian and Chinese admirals wondered if their fighter pilots had the same penis-drawing abilities. In fact, I bet even the chief of naval air forces, VAdm. Dewolfe "Bullet" Miller himself, got a chuckle out of "Sky Penis." Perhaps, even, it's something "Bullet" would have done as a young JO in an F/A-18A long before the advent of smartphones and social media. I wonder how many sky penises from days long ago we don't know about because YouTube didn't exist at the time.

Military humor has its very own style and parameters. Even in the same service the humor can be different among various communities. Navy surface warfare officers (SWOs), for instance, tend to have a very dark and dry sense of humor, whereas naval aviators and NFOs are more into hijinks and cheeky hilarity. All military humor has a touch of gallows in it, because in the military we deal in death. There was a Blue Angels pilot who once said that flying "isn't dangerous, but it's inherently unforgiving." We have rules to follow. Weather, Murphy, and physics always get a vote. If you violate the rules of weather and physics or leave any room for Murphy, the consequences will be swift and brutal. Many pilots, NFOs, and crewmen have died doing this thing we all love, and death flies wing every time we go up. When you live this life, whether training in California or flying in combat over Iraq, you come to look at life a little differently. It changes you, makes you stronger, or breaks you completely. It's not for everyone. Results may vary. All who try it will never forget it. This is why, I think, naval aviation humor has a common thread. The love of the job and the risk to life and limb create a common sense of humor from the shared trials, tribulations, and triumphs naval aviation has to offer. As such, we stare death in the face and laugh at him every time we laugh at ourselves.

SIMULATED!

Young student naval aviators in flight school are made to study emergency procedures, or EPs, for everything from engine failure to pilot-induced vertigo for the aircraft they train in. Students are made to remember the EPs verbatim and repeat them to their instructors during the flight brief and then perform the procedures in the aircraft when the instructor pilot, or IP, gives them a "simulated" emergency. One technique some IPs use is to induce a simulated malfunction without announcing it to the student, by manipulating the switches or the power lever from the back seat and waiting to see how long it takes the student to notice a change in the instruments.

Once the student notices the change, they tell the instructor, who then says, "Simulated." The student then has to quickly diagnose the problem and perform the memorized steps associated with the EP. "Simulated" is a dreaded word. There's enough pressure just to keep the airplane straight and level, let alone figure out what the emergency is and then recall from memory what you're supposed to do. That's a long explanation for setting up the following story. A brand-new Navy MH-60R pilot freshly minted from the Romeo FRS was riding as a passenger in his squadron mate's brand-new Dodge Charger on the I-5 through San Diego. The young nugget thought it would be funny to throw the gear shifter into idle and announce, "Simulated!" The unsuspecting driver had no idea what was going on, and almost lost control of the Charger at over 75 mph while trying to figure out why he no longer had control of the engine rpm. It's funny as a story only because the driver managed to regain control of the car and the young Romeo pilots didn't end up in the movie made for new drivers, *Red Asphalt 12: Blood All Over!*

There are many leather-bound books in rooms that smell of rich mahogany that detail everything you ever wanted to know about naval aviation. You can go to those rooms; visit the National Museum of Naval Aviation in Pensacola, Florida; ask Grandpa about the war; or find a PBS documentary on the subject. There's also this thing called Google, which can provide some details on this rarified profession. This book is not about giving you the history of naval aviation or describing the doctrinal use of naval air forces in war, but I'll give you a quick synopsis. Naval aviation is essentially sea- or land-based aircraft, aircrew, and all the aviation support functions that contribute to our nation's

An F-35B launches into the sunset from USS *Wasp*.

YATO is a badass! She's the first Marine Corps female F-35B pilot.

maritime security or offensive operations against an enemy on the sea or on land. In the United States this includes the aviation wings of the Navy, Marine Corps, and Coast Guard. There are pilots and NFOs in navies, coast guards, and marine corps all over the world, but this book is mostly about the pilots and NFOs in the US naval services.

CALL SIGN RULES OF ENGAGEMENT (UNOFFICIAL)

There are rules to the assignment of call signs, believe it or not. There have to be, given how much naval aviators and NFOs all hate their call signs when they first receive them. There has to be a code that ensures an assigned call sign is one that remains without hindrance from the bearer. So, without further ado, the following unofficial rules of call sign assignment apply:

1 You do not get to pick your own call sign. If you try, your call sign will be much worse than if you hadn't tried.

2 Your call sign can come from anything at all. You could be given a call sign for your looks, a play on your name, or something you've done while on liberty or while flying. Someone in your squadron may know something about you that's embarrassing, or your spouse could inadvertently reveal something embarrassing about your sex life to one of the other squadron spouses. Almost nothing is off limits. The possibilities are endless!

3 The more you hate your call sign, the more it will stick.

4 If you are found to like your call sign, as mentioned above, you may expect to receive a new one that you will definitely not like.

5 You are not allowed to unilaterally change your call sign. If you move across the country from one squadron to another, you can try to tell your new squadron that your call sign is something other than what you were originally assigned, but beware; the world of naval aviation is a small one. Someone somewhere will reveal your secret, and this will only bring you ridicule and shame.

6 Your call sign can be changed. For instance, if you received a lame call sign and then you do something utterly stupid and embarrassing, you will likely receive a new call sign. You'll probably miss your old one.

7 Call signs should be issued only to pilots, NFOs, and, in rare cases, aircrew. They should not be given to nonessential personnel such as SWOs or admin officers. Of course in *Top Gun*, Kelly McGillis's character did have the call sign Charlie, but you can't believe everything you see in the movies. This rule is probably the least concrete of all the rules on this list.

⬅★➡ NAVAL AVIATOR JOKES

How do you know a date with a naval aviator is halfway over? When they say, "But enough about me. Let's talk about airplanes."

How do you know there's a naval aviator in the room? They'll tell you!

KANGAROO COURTS, ROLL 'EMS, AND CALL SIGN REVIEW BOARDS

For the most part, naval aviators receive their call signs at kangaroo courts. You may have heard of kangaroo courts being used in oppressive countries where the accused are guilty until proven innocent. Squadron kangaroo courts are similar. First of all, all who are accused are called "guilty bastards" before, during, and after their "fair" trial. There are various court assignments given to members of the squadron. Kangaroo courts take many forms, and each squadron has its own customs and traditions. My only kangaroo court experiences are from my first fleet squadron, the Flying Tigers of Marine Medium Helicopter Squadron (HMM)-262. However, from speaking with other naval aviators, the general conduct and customs of a kangaroo court are pretty common throughout the fleet.

My squadron's kangaroo court consisted of several highly placed individuals who had absolute power. The CO of the Flying Tigers was referred to as the King Tiger, but never to their face. The King Tiger was addressed in formal terms usually reserved for royalty and high-court judges. The Big Kahuna was the official title given to the executive officer, who had less power than the King Tiger. However, the Big Kahuna served as both an advisor and enforcer for the King Tiger, and therefore the Big Kahuna's powers were many. Only the King Tiger could overrule the Big Kahuna.

There were also two litigators assigned, one for the prosecution and one for the defense. The prosecutor was the biggest smart-ass in the squadron and as such was usually very funny. The defense was usually the dumbest, dullest dude. I am not sure if the two litigators for the defense that I witnessed at my two kangaroo courts knew they were considered to be the dullest individuals in the squadron. Anyway, having the smart-ass as the litigator for the prosecution and the dumbass as the defense seemed fair. Over the course of a year, there were many opportunities for pilots to do something stupid, embarrassing, or humiliating, and these incidents were recorded in the Charge Book, which was kept in the squadron ready room. The Charge Book also recorded recommended call signs for individuals within the squadron who had either not yet received a call sign or who had done something worthy of a change in call sign.

The litigators either defended or prosecuted the actions identified in the Charge Book, or by grievances brought before the court in person. In defense or prosecution of their peers in the presence of the august body of the court, the two litigators risked jeering, ridicule, and removal if they failed to properly carry out their duties. The defense usually was shouted down before a valid argument could be presented, and the smart-ass prosecutor was at risk of being fined if he did not properly entertain the King Tiger and Big Kahuna. Justice took a back seat to entertainment.

As you have probably already guessed, much alcohol is consumed over the course of a kangaroo court's proceedings. Drinks were delivered by the "beer wenches," brand-new pilots to the squadron whose uniforms for the occasion consisted of something less than flattering to the male physique, such as the grass skirts and coconut bras my fellow nuggets and I wore at our first K-court. During my first kangaroo court, my fellow beer wenches and I were all men.

All others at the kangaroo court wore their flight suits, but there were very specific instructions on how the flight suit was to be worn. For instance, at my second kangaroo court we wore our flight suits unzipped to our belly buttons and without T-shirts. We were required to wear numerous bits of gold jewelry hanging from our necks, like we were 1970s gigolos. Additionally, we had to wear a black sock on our left foot and a white sock on the right under our flight boots. In our diagonally zipped pockets on our chests, we each carried the squadron challenge coin and exactly 262 yen (we were in Okinawa, Japan). Outlandish sunglasses and Elvis wigs were not required, but they were acceptable accessories to the aforementioned uniform regulations. If anyone failed to follow the instructions to the letter, they were fined a minimum of five dollars for each infraction. Failure to deliver cash on-site

led to other repercussions. I was a teetotaler, so during my second court I was naturally assigned as the designated driver. As such I carried a spare flight control rod, decorated in our squadron colors, with everyone's car keys attached to a ring at the top of the rod. The rod was 8 feet tall.

The proceedings consisted of a period where guilty bastards were fined for their misdeeds once they were deemed worthy of punishment by the Big Kahuna. Others were fined for not following the court's uniform regulations or the rules of the court. By the time call signs were assigned, the court was well oiled and the scene took on the appearance of Roman citizens watching as a gladiator asked Caesar whether or not to spare his defeated opponent's life. Call sign suggestions were shouted out, arguments erupted, and sporadic bursts of loud laughter indicated that someone's idea for a call sign was acceptable to the majority of the assembled sky devils.

As a young boy who aspired to be a Marine pilot one day, I remember coming up with what I thought would have made great call signs. I thought of such things as Buck or Razor or Buzz. I'm sure others thought of what they wanted their call signs to be too. I didn't get a very flattering call sign, and neither did any of the new guys I checked in to the squadron with. Eventually, we figured out that no one likes their call sign when they first get one. What matters most is that the members of the court find it funny, even if it's funny only when massive amounts of booze have been ingested. As the court proceedings wore on, and the members of the court grew more and more inebriated, the good order and discipline (what little was left) fell apart. There was a lot of laughter, pilots falling over drunk, spilled drinks, and even crashed plates. (The CO at my second K-court leaned against a cart stacked with dinner plates that collapsed, shattering the plates all over the floor of the Kadena Air Force Base officers club. I don't think we were welcomed back after that.) Many bad decisions were made, but the kangaroo court was more fun than you could shake a stick at. In our case, it was more fun than the Kadena officers club manager would have preferred.

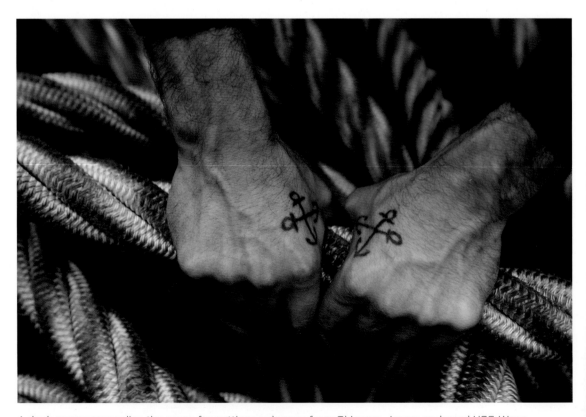

A deck crewman readies the ropes for getting underway from Okinawa, Japan, on board USS *Wasp*.

When the proceedings were finally concluded, the court adjourned to another drinking establishment where drinks flowed and women were pursued and flirted with. We were definitely poor guests and unwelcome sights to the Air Force officers at the Kadena officers club bar, trying to pick up on the nurses, defense school teachers, and WestPac widows. Squadrons from around the Navy and Marine Corps have similar proceedings, with their own fetishes and idiosyncrasies. Knowing what the kangaroo court is all about should provide you some insight as to why call signs are so incredibly funny and terrible at the same time.

Another tradition for call sign assignment is a practice at sea called "Roll 'ems." My buddy Dickens, a Navy Hornet pilot, provided the following description of a "Roll 'em" that included the Call Sign Review Board, or CRB.

Per squadron tradition, when a no-fly day was scheduled for the air wing (usually to allow the ship to conduct underway replenishment or do ship drills), the senior JO would request the skipper approve a Roll 'em night beginning at the conclusion of flight ops on the night before the day off. Once approved, the preparation would fall to the squadron duty officer for that day, and they would enlist the help of the other JOs for the various tasks required to make an epic movie night. This event was a big deal to the JOs assigned to facilitate it, and every effort was made to make the entire night perfect: from the plethora of snacks provided, to the movie selection (the higher the body count, the better), to the "tactical fade" of the premovie music finely synced with the dimming of the lights and the start of the film. No detail was left unaccounted for, lest the SDO and his or her minions be ridiculed mercilessly for their egregious disrespect of the sacred Roll 'em.

Roll 'em night began the morning of, with the SDO drawing "the Marquee" on one of the large whiteboards in the ready room. The marquee was meant to provide a clue as to the movie picked for the Roll 'em, but was not allowed to contain any words from the title. Creative SDOs would often create elaborate cartoons depicting scenes or characters from the film. Less talented SDOs would draw puzzles that could be deciphered in phases to guess the title, much like the puzzles under Lone Star beer bottle caps. For their part, the guessers trying to solve the puzzle were strictly forbidden from blurting their guess out loud, lest they spoil it for the rest of the squadron. The exception to this rule, for comedy's sake, was if the guess was patently absurd and would provide squadron mates with a good chuckle.

The SDO was also responsible for organizing all the FNG's proposed call signs onto a whiteboard to facilitate voting later in the evening and nominating three Duty Turds of the Day (DToDs). Traditionally, DToDs were characters on the ship who had somehow become persona non grata to the discerning aviators of our squadron. Sometimes it was a SWO who always took the last cookies at lunch. Other times it was a SWO who took all the best cereal off the snack rack. SWOs got it a lot. This dubious award would be voted on later during the festivities as well.

The goal was to have everything ready to go as soon as all the flight-related work was wrapped up. At the conclusion of flight ops that night, the SDO and his/her helpers would wrap up the day's busy work, ops summaries, and hour totals and account for all the classified material. Then, all the officers would begin to trickle in for the big show. Snacks were passed out. Reams of paper were crumpled, piece by piece, in order to make projectiles to throw at those who were deserving of such ire. Jocularity and frivolity ensued.

Once the wardroom was assembled, the skipper ceremoniously approved the commencement of the formalities and the SDO was charged with presiding over each new-guy CRB, wherein the FNG would be called up to the front and, through a very scientific accounting process, given his squadron-chosen moniker based on public approval (as measured in applause) for each offered call sign. Sometimes the lists of prospective call signs were quite long, and the process required multiple rounds of votes. When the lucky new guy was finally dubbed, he was formally presented to the squadron by the SDO with his new call sign, beaming with pride . . . then promptly forced to exit with a barrage of wadded-up paper.

The Duty Turd of the Day was voted on in a similar manner, and someone, usually one of the department heads (midlevel senior officers), was appointed to represent the fat SWO who stole the cookies and was justly punished with a stoning requisite of such heinous behavior, if only in effigy.

Finally, the skipper would declare it was time for the movie. But before it could start, the SDO was obliged to assign watch duties to various trusted agents in the crowd. These included Body Counter, Hot Girl Watch Officer, Lights Dimmer, and Sound Man, just to name a few. Prized among these extra duties was Realism Officer, whose job it was to shout out, with as much judgmental tonality as possible, "Not Real!," anytime something he or she deemed unrealistic occurred in the movie.

At the skipper's call of "3-2-1, Roll 'em!" the SDO and his team would simultaneously dim the lights, switch the sound from music to movie, and press play. This was a lot more difficult back then with the giant clunky DVD players and surround sound. God help you if you messed this process up . . . or if anyone had to watch even a second of credits.

WESTPAC WIDOW

A WestPac (Western Pacific) widow is a spouse who has inappropriate relations with people while their other half is deployed somewhere in the Western Pacific region. They can usually be spotted at enlisted clubs and officers clubs everywhere in California and Japan.

THE SORDID HISTORY OF CALL SIGNS

Apparently no one really knows the origin of call signs. Supposedly they were used in World War I by pilots from all nations involved as a way to build camaraderie or else to dehumanize their squadron mates, since pilots died at the cyclic rate in combat over the trenches of the Great War. Maybe British, French, Italian, American, and German pilots didn't take it so personally when their squadron mates died, since they never knew their real names to begin with.

When radio communications were introduced to aviation, ground controllers referred to the pilots by their nicknames because they could keep better track of whom they were talking to. Call signs really blew up in World War II, when tactical call signs were first used to communicate between aircraft. The first World War II call sign that comes to mind, at least for Marine aviators, is Greg "Pappy" Boyington. Pappy was the commanding officer of the famous Black Sheep of Marine Fighter Squadron (VMF) 214 (one of my dad's old squadrons), and he was so named because at thirty-two, he was a bit older than the rest of the pilots he commanded. There was a TV show made about Pappy and the Black Sheep in the 1970s. It was not historically accurate, but it was entertaining. After World War II, most naval aviators were routinely assigned call signs. Call signs filled two purposes: they were used for tactical communication between aircraft and to build camaraderie among men in the fraternity-like atmosphere of the ready rooms, wardrooms, and o'clubs of old.

In the old days, pilots and NFOs of all ranks gathered at officers clubs such as Cubi Point in the Philippines and favored off-base establishments such as Trader Jon's in Pensacola on Friday nights to drink, relax, and share stories and lessons from carrier aviation and aerial combat. Young aviators and NFOs could throw caution to the wind and ask questions of admirals and generals that would benefit them in the cockpit and professionally as they advanced in their careers. The aviators addressed each other by their call signs, and rank was not used. This was all part of the culture of naval aviation. Bonds were forged over beers and whiskey, and much laughter and fun was had. Then the bottom fell out.

TAILHOOK SCANDAL

Unfortunately, there have been naval aviators and NFOs who have taken the fun a little too far. The decline of the "Golden Era of Naval Aviation" began with the Tailhook scandal in 1991. From 1986, when *Top Gun* was released, until the 1991 Tailhook Convention, naval aviators were on top of the world. The world of SWOs was overshadowed by the larger-than-life daredevils of the sky who liked fast airplanes, fast women, and fast motorcycles. It all started to unravel when eighty-three women and seven men were sexually assaulted on the third floor of the Las Vegas Hilton Hotel in a Tailhook tradition that stretched back to the very beginning of the Tailhook association. Rowdy and drunk Navy and Marine aviators lined the walls of a long hotel hallway and waited for unsuspecting women to walk through. If the woman was attractive, a lookout would call out, "Clear deck!" If she was not, the lookout would call out, "Wave off!" Victims of this "tradition" were fondled, grabbed, and groped, and pieces of their clothing were ripped away as they tried to make their way through the unexpected gauntlet of rowdy aviators.

In some cases, women were lifted off their feet and passed down the hallway like a crowd surfer at a rock concert, often exposing their breasts or underwear. In the hotel rooms rented in blocks by the association, there were raunchy parties with hookers and strippers while porn videos played on TVs. Alcohol flowed endlessly. Two of the women who were assaulted were pioneers in naval aviation themselves, since they were some of the first women authorized to fly combat aircraft in the Navy. Witnesses to the carnage reported that the '91 Tailhook Convention paled in comparison to previous Tailhook conventions they had attended. Many of the younger pilots and NFOs who were interviewed during the investigation that followed claimed that they thought this behavior was condoned by the Navy, since it had gone on for so long and since senior officers had participated.

The annual Tailhook convention, which is still held today (although not nearly as debauched), is a gathering of pilots, NFOs, and aircrew who fly aircraft carrier–based airplanes. These airplanes vary in design and function, but they all have a tailhook, which catches the arresting cable on touchdown when the aircrew and machine land on an aircraft carrier. The Tailhook Association was founded in 1956, with the intent of gathering Navy and Marine carrier aviators together to share ideas, stories, and lessons learned. Additionally, it was formed as a sort of fraternity (at the time, there were no women in naval aviation). Camaraderie and esprit de corps were fundamental principles adhered to by the association. Over the years the Tailhook Convention's debauched after parties, where some pilots and NFOs wrecked hotel rooms and accosted women without fear of consequence, grew more and more riotous and out of control, especially as some of these aviators returned from combat tours in Vietnam.

There was clearly something wrong with the culture of naval aviation. It was definitely a boys club where women were not welcome. Since the association was sort of a fraternity, some of the ranks that filled it acted accordingly while at the convention among their peers and under the approving gazes of their superiors. In most cases the behavior of pilots and NFOs at the convention was good clean fun, and it built camaraderie and esprit de corps, but some engaged in ungentlemanly treatment of women, and this had gone on for far too long. At a time when women were coming to the fore and the rest of America was coming around to women's equality, the culture in naval aviation was way behind the power curve. Naval aviators were in for a very rude awakening.

When the story broke, the Department of Defense, the secretary of the Navy, and Congress launched investigations to determine what and who was to blame. It became a political circus. Congress was aided by the SWO community, determined to knock the brash aviation community down a notch or two after the post–*Top Gun* attention aviators so enjoyed. Rep. Patricia Schroeder (D-CO) took the lead in Congress and was determined to "break the culture" of naval aviation. That culture needed changes, but the politicians and policymakers went too far. The investigation turned into a witch hunt. Many Navy and Marine officers were justifiably fired or saw their career

The Machine! You'll read about the Machine later on.

progression come to a screeching halt, but there were many others who hadn't taken part in the nefarious activities in Las Vegas, but whose membership in the Tailhook Association made them guilty by . . . um . . . association; these officers also faced severe consequences. The o'club culture was also attacked. Most o'clubs were closed. Those that remained open were turned into "all hands" clubs.

Naval aviation changed to something almost unrecognizable to the old salts who flew off wooden-decked carriers or dodged surface-to-air missiles over Hanoi. There are still a couple of old-school watering holes around, such as the Iwakuni O'Club and the World Famous I Bar on NAS North Island, but most are just boring "all hands" clubs with historical pictures on the walls that no one still serving can relate to. Sadly, Trader Jon's was closed for good in 2003. All that remains of the storied Trader Jon's is a historical plaque that memorializes the former favorite saloon of instructors and student naval aviators, ranging back to 1941 and America's entrance into World War II. The camaraderie, salty career and flying advice, and enjoyment of being in the presence of your fellow naval aviators in such a relaxed and celebratory environment are hard to come by these days. Alas . . .

Many reasons have contributed to the decline of the good old days hanging out at the o'club on a Friday night. Bases aren't as isolated as they once were, which means naval aviators and NFOs have a lot more options for having fun on a Friday or Saturday night, and since 9/11, civilians can't just come on base to mix it up with pilots and NFOs at the o'clubs like they used to. Ever since the Department of Defense's crackdown on drunk driving, no one is willing to risk their careers over a couple of beers at the o'club before driving home. However, the Tailhook scandal was the initial volley in the war on naval aviation culture (warts and all), and the other factors described here were so much salt on the festering wound left in the wake of what happened at the Las Vegas Hilton in 1991.

JET GUY SHENANIGANS

I was introduced to the games that jet guys play to pass the time by the fighter pilots of VMFA-121, the "Green Knights." Usually at lunch or during card games, little games they played would come up, and someone would ask what the hell they were talking about. One game they played was called "Manchester," wherein a pilot would claim in a joking manner that they would do something ridiculous, like go talk to the commodore and "give him a piece of my mind" for a lame liberty policy. We all say silly things we don't mean in order to be funny. Once someone says something outlandish, someone else yells out, "Manchester!" The person who made the outlandish claim has two choices: (1) carry out what they said in jest or (2) buy a round of drinks for all assembled. On the ship, you had to submit to a slap in the face, since adult beverages aren't readily available. Two examples of this game that I witnessed: (1) during an Air Planning Board, there was a disagreement about something, and Scally threatened to call the ship's captain if he didn't get his way, if only in jest. BT yelled out "Manchester!," and Scally immediately called the ship's captain. "Hi sir, I am calling you because I lost a game and as a result I had to call you." The ship's captain didn't skip a beat. "Glad I could be of assistance, Scally!" (2) While in Thailand on Liberty, BT (who was the Manchester champion) picked up a package of ping-pong balls at a Family Mart and offered to give us a "Ping-Pong show" by shooting the ping-pong balls from his rear end. G-Roy immediately hit BT with, "Manchester!" You'll be happy to know that BT elected to buy a round of drinks. We were all a little disappointed that we didn't get our very own in-house Ping-Pong show. By the way, Manchester can be defeated by simply saying, "No Manchester!" before someone hits you with "Manchester!"

CALL SIGN SCANDALS

In addition to the Tailhook scandal, there have been two recent call sign scandals that have greatly affected the way call signs are assigned. Jet guys ruin everything (says the rotor guy). The Tailhook scandal, like the ones you'll learn about here, didn't affect just the jet community; they affected all communities (maritime patrol, transport, rotor wing, etc.). In 2012 at NAS Oceana in Virginia, there was a squadron admin officer who wanted to fit in. He pleaded with the pilots in his squadron to give him a call sign. Due to his somewhat effeminate mannerisms, the pilots put forth names such as "Gay Boy," "Cowgirl," and "Romo's Bitch." "Romo's Bitch" won the vote because Ens. Steven Crowston was a Cowboys fan. Crowston, a limited-duty officer who had previously been a chief, wasn't aware that they thought he was gay (he wasn't), and this was not the way he wanted to find out. And, as a non-naval aviator, he was not aware of the way call signs were used. He filed an inspector general (IG) complaint. The investigation determined that his call sign and the other suggestions amounted to sexual harassment.

In 2017, two African American naval aviators were kicked out of VFA-106, the East Coast fleet replacement squadron for F-18s, for substandard performance, but the two filed IG complaints because they believed their dismissal was racially motivated. They cited their call signs as examples of what they deemed as racial prejudice. One of the pilots was named "Radio" after the Cuba Gooding Jr. character in the movie of the same name. Whether racism was to blame or not, or whether or not the admin O was sexually harassed, may or may not be up for debate, but I would argue that a little more sensitivity to the sociopolitical environment on the part of the givers of these scandalous call signs may have saved the rest of us a lot of trouble. Regardless, the Navy was forced to make changes because both stories made the news. As a result, the chief of naval operations was compelled to institute command guidance on the protocol surrounding call sign assignment.

Like every other reactionary response, the new protocols went too far, and call signs just aren't as cool or fun as they once were. Whereas changes certainly needed to be made—no one should have a racially motivated call sign or feel sexually harassed—the changes to policy, which were a bit knee jerk, took "special trust and confidence" away from commanders in the assignment of call signs. Today, all call signs have to be approved at the group or even the wing level. People with eagles or stars on their collars now must take time out of their busy schedules to ensure that Lt. j.g. Schmucatelli's call sign doesn't embarrass the chief of naval operations.

CALL SIGNS TODAY

Due to the scandals outlined above, commanding officers have to be very vigilant with their junior officers to make sure that they aren't giving someone a call sign because of their race, religion, sexual orientation, sex, ethnicity, or any other reason that someone somewhere will find offensive. Additionally, call signs today shouldn't reference alcohol, sexual acts, or illegal activity, per official policy. While I agree that people shouldn't be singled out for whatever they identify as, I think there should be some leeway on call signs assigned for good fun and the purposes of camaraderie, whatever they may be. When an aviator takes the biggest woman in the bar home, and an NFO gets caught using a makeshift tampon, these things should not be off-limits for call sign assignment.

I said it earlier and I will say it again. This book has been very hard to write due to the scarcity of good call sign stories these days. The scandals and the extra scrutiny placed on commanders and aviators have greatly affected the ability of people to earn call signs the old-fashioned way: being stupid, looking funny, funny last name, etc. If sex and fecal matter are involved, then so be it! The stories I have gathered for you, dear reader, are meant to make you laugh and to show you another

side to naval aviation you probably didn't know existed. The simple truth is that people in the military are reflections of the societies they come from. Your military is nothing short of a reflection of you.

The high command, however, would have John and Jane Q. Citizen believe that people within the military are choirboys and choirgirls, who always go to church, never swear, and drink only moderately. The truth of the matter is that just like the society they come from, military members run the spectrum of naughty and nice. Today, service members are crushed for liberty violations, drunken hijinks, and other minor infractions that back in the old days would have been handled by a wise old NCO behind a shed. The admirals and generals today came up in the military during the 1980s and 1990s, before smartphones and YouTube. The shenanigans they got into make the worst NJP (nonjudicial punishment) cases today look like child's play. Compared to the good old bad days, today's military members really do look like choirboys and choirgirls when compared to their predecessors from the 1990s, 1980s, and all the way back to 1776. I recently had a discussion with a retired Navy captain, an F-14 pilot who was at the Tailhook convention in 1991. We were telling call sign stories and tales of the old days in such places as the Philippines and other parts of the Western Pacific, when I mentioned I was writing a book. He immediately chastised me for recording these stories. He was suddenly disgusted that someone would write a book full of such disgusting tales of drunkenness and debauchery. He said that I was gonna make naval aviators and NFOs look like degenerates. We aren't degenerates, folks. We are just like you, and when you put us all together in a room, we can sometimes act like middle-school kids. The saying goes that if you put a bunch of lance corporals or seaman recruits in a room together, they'll act like lance corporals and seaman recruits. If you put a bunch of generals or admirals in a room together, they too will behave like lance corporals and seaman recruits. Hijinks and humor, bad decisions, and tomfoolery are in our American blood. We are you and you are we.

Those helmets cost more than your house!

Naval aviators and NFOs today are cherubic compared to their forebears. However, we are held to a higher standard because we are supposed to represent the best of America. Believe it or not, regardless of drunken shenanigans and the occasional poo splatter, the military still represents the best of America. Being in the military is very hard work, and the consequences of not getting it right the first time can be deadly. If you join the military, any branch, you sign your life away to the American people, and the kind of person who is willing to do that is worthy of praise.

Just because this book is about naval aviators and NFOs in all of their disgusting and hilarious glory, it doesn't mean I think naval aviators and NFOs have a monopoly on service, sacrifice, and nobility in a life at the service of their country. But this book is about naval aviators and NFOs. So I bring you this glimpse of naval aviation humor and stories that could happen only in the bars and o'clubs, on the flight decks, and high in the skies frequented by naval sky devils, before they're lost to history forever.

If this book offends you, I sincerely apologize. I have done my best to weed out call signs and stories that were racist, sexist, homophobic, or prejudiced in anyway. I'm sure that 99 percent of call sign stories I heard did not fit any of the forbidden molds mentioned above (the 85% no-BS standard described below does not apply to this 99% statistic). The military is a more liberal and inclusive place than it has ever been. Yes, there are still prejudices among some members of the military, left and right, but most of us are pretty accepting people. Do your job and we don't care if you are attracted to people of the same sex, or you're purple with yellow polka dots. Do your job and you are worthy to be among us. If you have the right stuff, you should never be kept out because you're gay, identify as a broney, or like Justin Bieber. The days when call signs like the ones in this book exist are coming to a close and won't be around for long. It's a shame, really. We naval aviators and NFOs, while demented and crude, are some pretty funny people who can also put a 2,000-pound smart bomb into your bowl of Cheerios from 26,000 feet if you threaten the freedom-loving people of the world!

I have been warned that I may get into some trouble with some of the naval aviators and NFOs whose call signs appear in this book. To them I say I am sorry. I do not mean to get you into any kind of trouble, but I don't really foresee how these stories could be detrimental to you in the first place. Second, I suggest you embrace your call sign no matter how derogative or disgusting it may seem. Not everyone gets a call sign. Those who do are envied by those who don't. If you got a call sign, it means you were a naval aviator or NFO in the Navy or Marines, and you should be very proud of that.

All of that being said, you should take everything you read here with a grain of salt. About 85 percent of what you are about to read is 85 percent true. The remaining 15 percent is made up of embellishment, bull crap, half-truths, sea stories, fabrications, and outright lies. In all cases I have protected the innocent and not so innocent by omitting the guilty bastards' real names. For some of the more egregious selections in this book, I have made the call sign bearer an aircrew of an aircraft they didn't fly in. For instance, if an MH-60S pilot earned a call sign through something that could harm their career, reputation, or marriage, I may have fictitiously made them a naval flight officer in an E-2C Hawkeye. That'll fool 'em! I mean, between you and me, some of these call signs could get someone in a lot of trouble with their spouse or chain of command. If someone is associated with one or two of these call signs, born out of bad decisions made at, say, a strip club or something, they may face trial by court-martial followed by firing squad, and once their spouse is done with them, their command might have some questions. In most cases, the call sign bearer is properly matched with the aircraft they flew, but then again everything you've just read is only 85ish% true.

Up, up, and away on a Sea Hawk. Don't get blown away!

A NOTE ON ACRONYM CALL SIGNS

Excuse me, sir. Seeing as how the VP is such a VIP, shouldn't we keep the PC on the QT?
'Cause of the leaks to the VC he could end up MIA, and then we'd all be put out in KP.
—Robin Williams, *Good Morning, Vietnam*

I firmly believe that acronyms such as FUBAR and SNAFU greatly assisted the American dog face, aire-dale, squid, and jarhead in defeating the dirty Krauts and Japs during Dubbya Dubbya Two. WTF (Whiskey Tango Foxtrot) was originally used in Vietnam and greatly assisted in our efforts to defeat Charlie (mmm-hmm). In case you don't know, FUBAR stands for Fouled Up beyond All Recognition, and SNAFU stands for Situation Normal, All Fouled Up (the Fs in both of those acronyms don't really stand for "foul"). WTF stands for What the Frick (?!), but you already knew that because it's become part of the common ver-nacular. Acronyms are like a secret language in the military that only people in the military understand. After a while, if you stay in the military long enough, you can decipher what an acronym you've never heard before is, on the basis of the context it's used in and the most-common words represented by, say, the letter T (target, tactical, team, etc.) or M (mobile, military, missile, etc.).

We shorten everything into acronyms because the real names are too long and laborious to use in reports or on the radio. We use TLAs (three-letter acronyms) because it makes it all easier. I can TLA all day! We even have acronyms that have acronyms within them. It's like that common meme, "Yo dawg, I heard you like acronyms, so I put an acronym in your acronym so you can acronym while you acronym." When I was in Afghanistan in 2010, my team and I got around Helmand Province in an M-ATV, which stood for MRAP (mine-resistant armored personnel carrier)–all-terrain vehicle. For Marine officers, comical acronym alteration begins at the Marine Corps Basic Officer's Course (BOC), which is commonly referred to as TBS (The Basic School). My fellow second lieutenants and I sat around during downtime one day and came up with varied meanings of the initialism TBS. There was "Time between Saturdays," "The Big Suck," "The BS," and, my personal favorite, "Taggart's Butt Stinks" (I'm lactose intolerant, what?). It was our first sojourn into the possibilities that acronyms offer for comic relief.

As I formulated this book in my head, I had intended to have a chapter entirely dedicated to acronym call signs. The problem I ran into was that 85 percent of all call signs are made up of acro-nyms. As I collected these stories, I had to decide if a call sign warranted being in the acronym chapter or in another chapter because it was related to sex ("Sex and the Naval Aviator") or fecal matter ("The Crappiest Chapter You'll Ever Read"), etc. In the end, I decided to do away with the acronym chapter and divide the call signs therein among the other chapters of this book.

In this book you have read and you will read disparaging terms in reference to various groups of people. For instance, you may read words like Swabbo and squid, SHOE (Stupidest Humans on Earth), grunt or ground pounder, crayon-eaters, jet guy or pointy nosed, plopter pilot, shitter pilot, nonflying officers, skid kids, mouth breathers, knuckle draggers, and so on, and so on, and so on. All of these terms are used as part of the regular inter/intraservice rivalries that exist. Historically speaking, interservice rivalries have played out in dramatic ways, such as that be-tween the Army and the Navy during World War II. But here, these terms are used with endear-ment for my fellow naval brothers and sisters. They're just jokes, and I mean no harm or offense. It's just the way we in the naval services show our love for one another.

Portrait of a fighter pilot

CH-53E Sea Stallion (colloquially called a shitter) inbound for landing

CHAPTER 2

"Stupid is as stupid does." A very wise person said that. Most people, I think, view naval aviators and NFOs as many things, some good and some not so good, but I think most agree that naval aviators and NFOs are pretty smart. We'd have to be smart to be able to hurtle through the sky in a multimillion-dollar piece of machinery, right? Naval aviators and NFOs have to learn all about their aircraft's systems, instrument flying, rules and regulations that apply both to civilian and military aviation, and tons of other stuff just to be able to wiggle sticks or turn knobs. We must also be able to make quick decisions under pressure while engaging the enemy with our aircraft and weapons systems. There's a lot going on up there, believe you me.

Naval aviators and NFOs often speak to multiple agencies and aircraft via multiple frequencies. A naval aviator or NFO may be a flight lead, directing the actions not only of the aircraft they're in, but multiple other aircraft of various types and functions. We have to speak coherently and concisely to units on the ground, tactical air control agencies, and other aircraft while executing complex combat missions at night, all through a 40-degree NVG field of view with a grainy green image. We have to do one more thing, but I can't remember what it is. . . . Oh, I remember! We must also avoid turning Uncle Sam's multimillion-dollar aircraft into a multimillion-dollar lawn dart. Smart! Right?

Maybe, but smart people are capable of pulling off some of the stupidest crap you can imagine. In fact, our ability to do incredibly stupid things both in the air and on the ground is often aided by

Ospreys sit on the spots, lined up and ready to go, waiting for the signal to drop the hammer and spin.

Temperatures on the flight deck can get balls hot, and the humidity can bring a person down in ten minutes flat. Hydrate or die.

our brilliance. Usually, when we do something stupid it just damages our ego a little. Sometimes, though, it can cost a lot of money and even lives. Naval aviation is not dangerous, but it is very unforgiving, and so are our fellow naval aviators when we screw it up. There are no serious incidents reported in this book, but some of us have earned our call signs the hard way, and we've never forgotten how we earned them. It doesn't mean we don't continue doing stupid things, however. If you ask a naval aviator or NFO what their call sign is, and they claim they don't have one yet because they haven't done anything stupid, they will likely be corrected by someone else who will say that they've done plenty of stupid things—they've just never been caught.

Drater: An MH-53 pilot who was, well, special for all the wrong reasons earned a PC call sign that was meant to prevent the easily offended from being offended while adequately depicting the kind of special he was. He was called Drater. It's retard spelled backward, because spelling retard backward isn't offensive. Right?

BRIK: A mild-mannered and affable E-2C NFO got lost in Pusan after a night of heavy drinking with his squadron mates. When liberty expired that night, he failed to make it back to the ship. His squadron mates went out the very next morning to search for their wayward chum and found him listlessly wandering through a street market, with no recollection of what had happened the night before. Luckily for him, his cell phone pictures bore witness to his nocturnal adventure. He'd apparently had one hell of a good time. Fortunately for him, he was a very affable guy and he made friends in every bar he visited during his solo journey through Pusan. Unfortunately for him, he was placed on liberty restriction for a month and thereafter required a liberty buddy whenever he left the ship. BRIK stands for Buddy Required in Korea.

G-BAC: It may be difficult to imagine that in the world of naval aviation, one may occasionally come across some pretty type A, alpha male, chauvinistic personalities, but it does occasionally happen. One such mansplainer considered himself to be the Ace of the Base, the finest F-18 pilot the world had ever known. He claimed that no one could beat him in 1v1 air combat maneuvering (ACM) practice. He was, after all, the ace of the base (a legend in his own mind). Then one day he came across a bandit in the form of a desert-painted F-16 with Navy markings from one of the Navy's aggressor squadrons. The unknown F-16 pilot "waxed his tail," in the parlance of dogfighting, taking a little bit of the chip off the self-described ace of aces' shoulder. Turns out the mystery F-16 pilot was a woman. Girl power and feminism notwithstanding, the mystery pilot who happened to be a woman was a damn good fighter pilot who could show a Neanderthal F-18 pilot a thing or two about dogfighting. It was pretty humbling to the Navy F-18 pilot in our story. G-BAC stands for Gunned by a Chick. Not a particularly PC call sign, but that chick put G-BAC in his place. That was probably good enough for the mystery woman behind the controls of a desert-painted F-16 with Navy markings. For your edification, Navy and Marine Corps aggressor squadrons fly aircraft with aerial capabilities that are similar to Russian and Chinese fighter aircraft to help Navy and Marine Corps fighter pilots hone their ACM skills.

VILLAINS ON THE CARRIER

There are mythical villains that lurk in the shadows and create havoc and mayhem wherever they go on the ship. Below is my description of these sinister evildoers. The four horsemen of the apocalypse on the carrier are the Blue Falcon, Double Dragon, Good Idea Fairy, and Chain Monster.

The Blue Falcon is sort of the leader of all shipboard villains. The Blue Falcon's superpower is screwing over everyone around them (Blue is code for "buddy," while Falcon is code for the F word, since the common vernacular is buddy f**ker). They're the guy or gal, for example, who does something stupid out in town, which results in the Good Idea Fairy coming up with some new ridiculously stupid liberty policy, like requiring everyone to always have a liberty buddy whenever they leave the ship. Some believe that Blue Falcon and Double Dragon are one and the same, but no one knows for sure.

Speaking of Double Dragon, this disgusting creature from the sewers causes the double whammy of diarrhea and projectile vomiting . . . at the same time. The Double Dragon is not the microbial dot that causes you to get so intimate with the toilet bowl you think about naming it after a favorite aunt or uncle. No, they're the greasy little dirt bag who takes a dump, gets it on their hands, and then doesn't bother washing their nasty paws before walking around and spreading their microbial crap all over the ship.

Everyone's least favorite villain is the Good Idea Fairy. This sinister little creep is the genius that comes up with good ideas for operations, training, planning, etc., and they usually do so at the last minute, requiring all to jump through fiery hoops to make it happen. Their ideas are crazy enough that they just might work! They usually don't. They also come up with lame rules for liberty or laundry or whatever. Good Idea Fairies either occupy the highest staterooms of power on the ship, sliming around at some headquarters, or they are the power broker's little lackeys, always nipping at others' feet and whispering sweet nothings into the boss's ear. They work really well with Blue Falcon. It's like the Good Idea Fairy and the Blue Falcon are a dynamic duo, fighting happiness and common sense wherever they go.

Last, there is the Chain Monster. This spidery little douchebag wanders around at night on the flight deck, dragging chains, dropping them, picking them up, and dropping them again before dragging them some more and repeating the process. They usually do this directly above your stateroom at 0200, when you have a 0530 brief for a 0700 launch. Most of the officers sleep directly under the flight deck. The Chain Monster hates the officers sleeping in their comfy staterooms directly below while they are walking around the flight deck at night doing who knows what! They have lots of chains to drag and drop, but zero concern for your crew rest.

You see, the villains on the ship are actual people. We don't always know who they are because they can be sneaky little bastards. Sometimes, as in the case of Double Dragon, they are legion. Sometimes you might be the villain and you don't even know it. Usually, the villains know who they are but don't care if they screw up liberty for everyone or get the whole ship sick. The ship's villains are super douchebags with super douchebag powers.

There is one last villain worth mentioning who is disgusting and demented, but not as detrimental to morale as the abovementioned villains, and therefore is not included as a horseman of the apocalypse. I speak, of course, of the "Phantom Shitter." Somehow this is a naval aviation tradition that spans the entire history of our beloved institution. Someone on the carrier sneaks around at night and lays turds in very public places (e.g., the ready room, the passageway outside the air boss's stateroom). The Phantom Shitter has struck again! If you've ever seen the movie *Flight of the Intruder* or read the book of the same name by Stephen Coonts, the Phantom Shitter plays a key role in the plot. I highly recommend you see this movie for a full understanding of this truly demented individual.

CATS: All CH-53 pilots in the Marine Corps are familiar with the acronym CAPTS. This acronym helps Marine shitter pilots remember the first couple of steps in the emergency procedures for 85 percent of emergencies that can occur in the 53. In the NATOPS pocket checklist for the CH-53, those procedures look like this:

An MH-60S leaps into the air from the deck of USS *Wasp*.

What's the deadliest aviation payload known to man? A squad of Marines in the back of an Osprey. Yut!

1 Collective: maintain Nr
2 Airspeed: as required
3 Pickle: external load as required
4 Tanks: jettison as required
5 Speed control levers: as required (shut off affected engine, conditions permitting)

Since these steps are supposed to be memorized, they appear in bold print in the NATOPS pocket checklist. In certain emergencies, the most critical step is to pickle the external load, since it reduces the load requirement on the engines. This particular step may convert a "power required exceeds power available" situation into a "power available exceeds power required" one! Such was the case when a CH-53E was lifting from an LZ in Okinawa, Japan, with an underslung load of concrete barriers. For whatever aerodynamic fluke reason, the external load began swinging wildly toward the tail rotor. The crew chief frantically called out "PICKLE! PICKLE! PICKLE!" The pilot at the controls immediately started completing the steps for the emergency, but when he got to the third step, he messed up. Instead of mashing down on the pickle switch on the cyclic with his thumb, he mashed down on the cyclic trim switch instead. He continued with the rest of the steps but failed to complete the most crucial one. He failed to pickle the load. Luckily, the copilot recognized the missed step and hit the pickle switch on his own cyclic, saving the aircraft and crew, but not saving the pride of the pilot at the controls. CATS is simply the CAPTS acronym without the P for "Pickle."

Wedge: Harrier pilots are supposed to be pretty smart. In fact, Marine pilots who scored the highest at flight school usually got selected for the Harrier because it was more difficult to fly than the F-18. Somehow this guy, who seemed to lack the mental acuity required to be a Harrier pilot, got through. A Wedge is the simplest tool known to man.

Twister: WARNING! This story may lead men to feel a bit of vicarious pain. While training at Nellis Air Force Base in Vegas, a young Harrier pilot went out for a night on the town with his squadron mates. It was his very first visit to Las Vegas. For reasons no one to this day can explain, the young Harrier pilot somehow ended up with testicular torsion. Don't know what that is? It's when a man's balls wrap around themselves in a most excruciatingly painful way. Usually happens to guys with especially low hanging fruit. So out of sympathy for his plight, his squadron mates gave him this call sign to make sure he never forgot his first night in Sin City.

Jared: A P-3 pilot, described as "bat guano crazy" by the teller of this tale, was a little wrapped around the axle about most things on any given day. When the crew of a P-3 was getting ready to depart Hawaii after a six-month deployment there, they all popped into the base Subway for a couple of sandwiches for the long trip home before heading out to the flight line. Before departing Hickam Air Force Base for their eventual destination in Point Mugu, California, the crew was given a brief from an Air Force officer about the agricultural inspection they could expect to receive once they arrived in California, and what they were and were not allowed to bring with them to California. The list of prohibited items included any kind of flora or fauna. The pilot in our story lost her mind because of the lettuce in everyone's Subway sandwiches. Her crew laughed it off, thinking she was only joking. When they realized she was sincerely concerned about being arrested for international lettuce smuggling, they tried to calm her down. The obvious solution, they explained, was to just eat the sandwiches and all the lettuce prior to arriving in California, which was already the plan. This course of action failed to assuage the concerns of their fearless leader. I guess she was concerned about having to provide a stool sample or undergo a cavity search upon arrival. She insisted that the lettuce in all of the sandwiches be removed at once, and she then carried said lettuce to a trash can in a nearby hangar. For her due diligence in ensuring that no illegal lettuce smuggling occurred on her aircraft ("Not on my watch!"), she was awarded the call sign "Jared," after that Subway guy.

Snowden: We all know who Snowden is; one man's traitor is another man's patriot. Sometimes in naval aviation, too much information is shared in the presence of people it shouldn't be shared with. A cobra squadron was all set to have their Cobra court, similar to a kangaroo court but for AH-1W pilots. The difference between a kangaroo court and a Cobra court is that there is a lot more knuckle dragging and mouth breathing at a Cobra court. A young captain, who was due to receive a new call sign at the Cobra court, was giving the commanding officers of the squadron and the Marine air group a ride back to base from the rifle range. The car ride was long and quiet. Too quiet. The captain did not like uncomfortable silences and decided to strike up a conversation with his CO:

"Sir," he said, "we're all set for the Cobra court!" What Capt. Eager Beaver did not know was that the squadron CO had neglected to tell the MAG CO about the Cobra court.
The squadron CO said, "Good, we'll talk about it later."
The MAG CO, probably curious as to why this was the first he was hearing of the Cobra court, asked, "When's the Cobra court?" Before the squadron CO could get a word in edgewise, the captain announced that the Cobra court was planned for that very night!
The squadron CO said, "Thank you, captain; we'll talk about this later!"
The MAG CO pressed the issue. "Tell me about what you have planned." The young captain, failing to pick up on what the squadron CO was putting down, began to go into detail about the alcohol purchased, the venue, the entertainment, etc. The squadron CO, a touch of frustration in his voice, repeated, "Thanks; we'll talk about this LATER!" See, tradition holds that the squadron CO should have invited the MAG CO to attend the Cobra court. I don't know, maybe the MAG CO was a buzzkill or something. It was a long, awkward

An MV-22B inbound for fuel

car ride back to base. Talk about uncomfortable silences! So Captain so-and-so spilled the beans to the MAG CO. Snowden spilled the beans too.

Kaepernick: You may or may not be familiar with the NFL football player who protested the treatment of Black people in the United States by taking a knee during the singing of the national anthem at the beginning of NFL football games. There was a Marine CH-53E pilot very close to Kaepernick's heart, who engaged in some serious preflighting before arriving at his squadron's Marine Corps birthday ball. He may have done a tad too much preflighting, however. During the playing of the national anthem and the Navy and Marine Corps hymns, the young pilot, in full dress blues, had to take a knee because he was too drunk to stand. To make matters worse, he was part of the sword detail in the opening ceremony, so it wasn't as if he could just go to the back and take a knee. He was taking a knee for all to see, just like his hero Kaepernick. You gotta fight for your right to party, man!

Spam: A new CH-46E pilot checked in to his squadron. Within a few weeks of checking in, he started complaining about the command via email to some of his flight school buddies stationed on the same base. He wrote an email to his fellow junior officers but mistakenly sent the email to everyone on the air station, including his entire chain of command, all the way up to the wing commander. He spammed them. Haha . . . get it? Probably didn't work out very well for him.

Re-Todd: A guy in an MH-60S squadron had a hard time keeping up with his peers, although he turned out to be a pretty good pilot. He wasn't mentally challenged, so to speak, but he was definitely challenged. His name was Todd.

Ready! Step! Deck crew conduct firefighting drills.

⬛ IT'S LEAKING!

The CH-46E is known for a lot of things, but if you're a grunt who has ever flown in the back of one, the thing you probably remember most is all of the hydraulic fluid everywhere inside the cabin. You probably remember how slick the cabin's deck was, or how occasionally you'd have a drip of reddish hyd fluid glide down your shoulder or the back of your shirt. You may even have become concerned enough to let the crew chief know that the aircraft had sprung a leak, which to you may have been particularly disconcerting since you were in the back of this leaky vessel out over the ocean blue, with water, water everywhere, and not a drop you wanted to crash in. The conversation you had with the crew chief probably went something like this: "Hey dude, the bird's sprung a leak?" The crew chief, after taking a cursory glance in the direction you pointed, probably responded with "Nah, dude, it's all good. It's when she stops leaking that we have a problem!" I mean, the crew chief wasn't wrong. The leaking is how you knew there was still hydraulic fluid in the tank!

BANJO: A nugget showed up to a Navy F-18 squadron deployed on one of America's aircraft carriers. He met his new squadron on the pier in Hong Kong when they pulled in for a port visit. After getting checked in and as soon as liberty was sounded, his new squadron mates took the nugget out for a good time in Hong Kong. The new guy got absolutely smashed. On the liberty boat back to the ship, he was challenged to jump overboard for kicks and grins. A collection was taken up, raising twenty-seven dollars for the young lad if he was willing to make the leap. Alcohol sometimes allows one to do things that one wouldn't otherwise do. So, Nick the new guy jumped in. One of the other pilots yelled out, "Bring her around! Nugget jumped overboard." That's how the call sign BANJO was born. That's one hell of a way to introduce yourself to your new squadron.

NASA: Let the record show that MH-60 "Romeo" pilots have a reputation for being the SWOs of naval aviation. More than a few of them are a bit geeky and can be a little too rigid. These are the only pilots that surface warfare officers can really see eye to eye with. The MH-60R pilot in our story met all the criteria of your stereotypical Romeo pilot, but he was lacking the most important mental asset that any naval aviator, even Romeo pilots, hold essential to being a good pilot. He was just not gifted with what aviators refer to as situational awareness. He had none. It wasn't his fault; it just was what it was. Not to foreshadow the direction this is going, but he didn't get this call sign for being smart enough to be an astronaut. He didn't need to apply to be an astronaut, because his head was already in outer space. He was tested and the test results indicated that he had "no apparent situational awareness" (NASA).

SNITS and **SPITS**: Two guys showed up to a P-3 squadron at NAS Whidbey Island in Washington State, and the two became fast friends. One of them was a pilot and the other an NFO. They were like two peas in a pod. They even looked alike, with the exception that one was blond haired and the other was light brown haired. Among a number of defining characteristics they had in common was an important one; they were both subpar in the cockpit. So much so that they both failed their NATOPS check rides after having barely passed their NATOPS closed-book exams. Together they were the Stupidest NFO in the Squadron and the Stupidest Pilot in the Squadron. Someone has to be the worst.

BAGS: This call sign was earned before the bearer was even in the Navy. While a Navy ROTC midshipman at some college, the future "BAGS" attended the Indianapolis 500. Camping overnight on

the grounds of the famous raceway, the midshipman and his friends were having a good time until one of them was attacked without warning by four thugs. Our hero jumped into action and chased away the attackers. His friend announced that the thugs had taken his wallet and cell phone, so the midshipman gave chase. Catching up to one of the thieves, our hero pounced, managing to recover the stolen wallet and cell phone. Suddenly a shot rang out. Someone had shot the midshipman in the back while he was grappling with the thug on the ground. Once again our hero sprang into action. He stood up and confronted the shooter. The shooter, who couldn't believe the man he'd just shot was standing menacingly in front of him, chose to run instead of shooting again. Fortunately, our hero eventually recovered. After graduating from college, the midshipmen joined the Navy. While trying to pass the Navy's pistol qualification, he twice failed to meet the minimum score before finally earning his shooting ribbon. Turns out he was Better at Getting Shot than he was at shooting. BAGS still carries the bullet in his intestines to this day.

WALLE and **Eva**: If you're familiar with the Pixar movie *WALL-E*, then you know that his girlfriend was a killer robot named Eva. If not, there's this thing called Disney+. We'll start the story with WALLE. A Marine EA-6B pilot tended to lean a bit left politically, and he was not shy about sharing his political views. His buddy, an EA-6B NFO named Scally (short for Scallywag), thought long and hard as to what to call his liberal friend and wracked his brain for a call sign. He eventually landed on WALLE, but he didn't quite know which words to use to fill in the acronym. Scally thought to himself, "Well, he's as white as a newborn white baby's bottom. He's a leftist, and as such, a liberal, and he's a bit elitist." Then it came to him: White Ass Leftist Liberal Elitist. WALLE! Then there's

Eva. The EA-6B NFO who would come to be named Eva was a stocky, corn-fed country boy and former college football player. He was also new to the squadron. During a night of drinking, the new NFO challenged WALLE to see who could shoot a shot glass of whiskey and then down a beer the fastest. WALLE was a scrawny fellow, so most of the squadron put their money on the NFO. Much to the surprise and chagrin of the guys who put their money on Mr. Corn-Fed, WALLE absolutely crushed the new NFO, then did it again during a rematch. WALLE made the new NFO his little bitch, you know, like Eva was to WALLE.

BLIMP: After completing a seven-month deployment to Afghanistan with his squadron, a mild-mannered farm kid from Ohio, who flew Marine CH-53Es, returned to his apartment in downtown San Diego only to discover that someone had moved in while he was gone. His apartment was a disaster. It smelled like "the worst bathroom in Scotland." All of his valuables were gone, and there was trash everywhere. When he went into his bedroom, he discovered a large Black homeless woman asleep in his bed. She was wearing his clothes. When he woke her up, she leapt from the bed and attacked, beating the ever-living crap out of him. Welcome home, Marine! He managed an escape to call the cops. When Five-O finally arrived, the woman claimed that the apartment was hers. It turned out that the woman had previously lived in the apartment with her ex-boyfriend, and she had an envelope with her name above the address to prove it. The cops initially believed her, much to the chagrin of the traumatized Marine shitter pilot. Eventually, the fuzz figured out who the current tenant was, and the woman was taken away for mental evaluation and processing for criminal trespassing. The mild-mannered Marine pilot from Ohio probably needed a little mental evaluation himself after

An MV-22B is readied for launch from the deck of USS *Wasp*.

such a traumatic homecoming. Of course, when his squadron mates heard this terrible story, they knew there was a call sign in there somewhere. At some point during the telling of his traumatic tale, he said, "There was a Black Lady in My Place!"

CROSSWORDS IN THE WARDROOM

Cherub to the room: "Anyone know the answer to 38 down?"
Someone in the room who was not doing the crossword puzzle: "What's the clue?"
Cherub: "The clue is 'alcohol problem or stressful job.' P-I-L-O-T doesn't fit."

Preacher: This call sign is usually given to Mormons or other religious types in the squadron. In this case it was given to a guy who had recently been married. On his wedding day the priest failed to show, so "Preacher," an ordained minister in the Church of the Flying Spaghetti Monster (it's a real religion) officiated at his own wedding.

SAWDUST: When you first check in to a squadron, you may need a little time to get situated, figure out your place, and become proficient in your aircraft and ground duties. Some guys can do all three at the same time. You can count on them to handle their responsibilities, be where they need to be on time, and take time to study and learn everything they can about the naval aviation profession. Then there's this guy, a Marine CH-53D pilot, who couldn't be relied on to zip his fly up, let alone do simple tasks required of copilots in the aircraft. He was terrible in the cockpit and couldn't find his way out of a wet paper bag. He needed constant supervision. You might say he was situationally unaware. SAWDUST stands for Situational Awareness Weak, Doesn't Understand Simple Tasks. Another suggestion was SIRE, for Simple Instructions Require Explaining. SAWDUST sounded better, I guess. It's one of those call signs that you make a lie about so you don't have to tell anyone why you earned such a notorious moniker. I wouldn't know about that . . .

STAB: A Marine F/A-18 pilot took his new wife to Hawaii for their honeymoon. He rented a Cessna 172, filled it with rented SCUBA gear, and took his bride out for a day of adventure in the land of Aloha. Out over the water with nowhere to land, the engine quit and he couldn't get it to start again. He had no choice but to ditch. It was a textbook ditching. He and his wife escaped the sinking aircraft and were rescued by the Coast Guard. They were just fine. All the SCUBA gear, however, went down with the airplane. When he returned to his squadron and told his tale, someone smugly told him that he Should've Taken a Boat.

ZEUS: This is not the all-powerful god of Greek mythology. No, this was a Navy MH-60 pilot who just could not be left unsupervised. He just couldn't be bothered. If no one was supervising him, he was not doing what he was paid to do. For instance, he was supposed to study to be a helicopter aircraft commander. Nope, too much work. He was supposed to accomplish his daily tasks in his ground duties. Nope, too much bother. ZEUS stands for Zero Effort, Under Supervision.

Brick: A young Mennonite decided not to return to the farm as the end of his Rumspringa approached. Instead, he ran away from home in search of his dreams but ended up falling into the seedy world of naval aviation. His life spun wildly out of control. In the end he became a lowly MH-60S pilot on the mean streets and in the skies of Norfolk, Virginia. He still held on to some of his Mennonite ways, though, which essentially translated to him being a really weird dude. His

physical appearance and personality quirks reminded his squadron mates of the character "Brick" from the movie *Anchorman*. That's not the best call sign story ever, but the young runaway Mennonite did drop some Mennonite knowledge on his squadron mates one day in reference to something that requires little effort. He said, "That's as easy as drowning a kitten in a boot full of milk!" Naturally, his squadron mates asked for an explanation. It was just a Mennonite colloquialism, but it had a very dark background story. Apparently, when Mennonite kids get bored, they fill a boot with milk so that an unwitting kitten will stick its head in for a refreshing drink. The problem is that the little kitten drowns because it lacks the strength to back its way out of the boot. This causes deranged little Mennonite psychopaths to laugh maniacally. Needless to say, there was a collective look of "What the actual hell?" on the faces of all of Brick's squadron mates when he explained this twisted backstory to a weird Mennonite saying.

CRG (pronounced Surge): A Marine MV-22B pilot wasn't very good at reading in public to begin with, but he was especially illiterate when he'd had too much to drink. At his first kangaroo court, he was given a less than memorable call sign. However, when he stood up to read aloud a charge sheet that he had written for one of his pals, he botched it so badly that the squadron CO leaned over to the XO and asked if the kid could actually read. Someone in the crowd, who was not altogether brighter than the young illiterate Marine officer, blurted out, "Call sign, Surge! Can't Read Good!" It seemed to fit.

The Det OIC for the MH-60S Boonie Sharks smiles for the camera before departing for home at the end of a deployment on USS *Wasp*.

Asphalt: A nugget Marine EA-6B Prowler pilot was tasked with conducting an engine run-up so that the mechanics could make adjustments to the engines. The aircraft was towed to a section of pavement not normally used for such run-ups. The young pilot ran the engines up to military power on the signal from the lineman. Suddenly the lineman told the pilot to cut the engines, with frantic hand and arm signals. The nozzles on the Prowler have a slight downturn to them, and with the engines in military power his jet exhaust had caused the pavement to melt and bend back on itself. There was a large asphalt taco lying on its side, directly behind the jet exhausts. Once the jet was shut down, the young pilot dutifully called base operations to let them know what happened. He was told not to worry about it because that area was not often used. Then he told his XO what had happened and how base ops had said it wasn't a big deal. The XO told him not to worry about it. So, a bit in-credulously, the young pilot went home, surprised that he wasn't in any sort of trouble. When he showed up to work the next day, he discovered that the thing that wasn't a big deal was in fact a very big deal. After all the dust settled from the aftermath of the asphalt disaster, a new call sign was born. Since he was responsible for the melting of the asphalt, he was given the call sign Ass Fault, as in "It was his own ass fault." Get it? It sounds like asphalt, but it's spelled like ass fault . . . anyway. . . . The wing commanding general didn't think it was funny, and told the squadron CO to come up with something less offensive. So instead of changing it completely, the CO had the young pilot change his call sign to Asphalt.

THE TRAPPED F-35 PILOT

The ship, or boat, can be a confusing place. It has passageways and ladder wells going every which way, and a confusing numerical convention written on all the bulkheads (walls) to help you get where you want to go. When the tool to get you there is confusing, and you're already confused, it can be a little disorienting. The wardroom is where the officers on the ship eat their meals. It's not particularly confusing to get there, to go into, or to leave. Not to most people anyway.

There was one F-35 pilot who found the wardroom very confusing when he went in late one night for a cup of coffee. The wardroom doubles as a conference room. All kinds of briefs and meetings go on in there, because room on the ship is at a premium. When the wardroom is used for meetings, there are two plastic placards with Velcro attached that stick to the outside of the doors. They read "Meeting in Progress. Enter Only in Emergency." The sign is usually ignored. I mean, if you want coffee or cereal, where else are you gonna get them? I digress. When there is not a meeting in progress, the placards are stuck to the inside of the doors. They are big and red and hard to miss.

The F-35 is the most advanced fighter jet known to man. Its capabilities are beyond amazing, and our enemies should be very afraid. The pilots who fly them are the best of the best. Millions of dollars are spent to train them to fly these spaceship-like jets and bring freedom to the op-pressed people of the world, whether they want freedom or not. The F-35 pilot in our story was one of these chosen few. He was screened for intellectual abilities, acuity, physical endurance, the ability to solve complex problems quickly, and being able to make split-second decisions that could mean the difference between life and death. He had the Right Stuff! However, it wasn't enough to get him through this late-night predicament.

Having obtained his coffee, he went to exit the wardroom through one of three doors. The wardroom sits between two main passageways, and there are doors on either side of the ward-room that lead to these p-ways. There's a third door that people use to sneak into the wardroom during meetings to get coffee or noncarbonated soda from the soda machine. These three doors

Those big jet-launching aircraft carriers don't have hovercraft, but USS *Wasp* does. Neat!

Going my way, sailor? An MV-22B on short final for USS *America*.

offered quick escape to our uber-capable F-35 pilot. As he approached the door he entered the wardroom through, he saw the red placard: Meeting in Progress, Enter Only in Emergency. Thinking there was a meeting happening in the p-way that he wasn't invited to, he performed an about-face and went for the door on the other side of the wardroom. It too had the red placard. He could not believe his luck. There must be meetings going on in both p-ways!

He approached a couple of SWOs enjoying a late-night poker game and asked them how he was supposed to leave the wardroom. The SWOs didn't understand what he was asking. One SWO just pointed to the door and said he could exit through there. The F-35 pilot looked confused. He could not go through there because of the bright-red placard posted on the door. The SWO took the young F-35 pilot by the hand and showed him that the placards were meant to be obeyed only when they were on the other side of the door. Rest easy, America! The defense of our nation is in the hands of the best of the best!

Balloon: This call sign was short lived. While learning how to fly the Harrier at the West Coast Harrier Fleet Replacement Squadron in Yuma, Arizona, a young, newly winged student had somehow become separated from his formation partner while flying instruments in the goo. At the time there was a weather balloon that floated on a tether at 12,000 feet aboveground near Yuma. It had flashing lights so pilots could see and avoid the balloon and its tether. By the time his formation partner had landed at the air station, unbeknown to him, the young Harrier student pilot saw flashing lights through a hole in the clouds. He tried to form up on what he thought was the other jet in his flight. He was baffled as to why his radio calls on the interflight frequency were going unanswered. It's really hard to fly formation on a weather balloon, but this guy somehow managed. He didn't make it through the Harrier FRS, unfortunately. I'm sure he was an awesome supply officer, though.

SNATCH/SNITCH: There is an MH-60S squadron in Guam called Helicopter Sea Combat Squadron 25. They're known as the Island Knights. They stand a twenty-four-hour alert for search and rescue (SAR) and often get called out to rescue someone in distress both on land and sea. One brand-new copilot was fortunate enough to be called out to a rescue on his very first time standing the alert. Somewhere between Tinian and Saipan, a Chomoran fishing boat was taking on water and needed rescuing. Upon arriving at the scene, the brave MH-60S crew discovered a Chomoran boat that seemed to fit the description of the distressed vessel in question. Other boats nearby appeared to be pointing in the direction of the distressed boat, which seemed to correlate with what the SAR crew were seeing. They entered into a hover over the "distressed" boat, and, after a brief argument with the fishermen on board, the rescue swimmer hoisted them all into the aircraft. The SAR crew were heroes, and the young copilot was pleased as punch to be a part of the crew that rescued these thankful Chomoran fishermen. There was one little problem, though—just a slight oversight. They rescued the wrong guys, and the boat they rescued them from was lost at sea when left adrift by the departing SAR helicopter. The Chomoran fishermen sued the Navy for the replacement cost of their boat. The aircraft commander already had a call sign, and very shortly after the incident he moved on to another squadron somewhere else. The copilot was left to bear the brunt of the embarrassment. The original call sign he was given was Snatch, since the hapless crew had essentially kidnapped the unwitting Chomoran fishermen. However, his squadron mates didn't think the proposed call sign was fitting. You see, the copilot who might have been named Snatch had a habit of tattletale telling on all of his squadron mates for great and minor misdeeds. Even the CO started calling him Blue Falcon. One of the HACs came up with something a little more fitting. His call sign became SNITCH; Saved No one, Instead Took Chimorans Hostage. SNITCH was more about the tattletale telling.

SNITCHES get stitches.

Note: Chamoran fishing crews have been known to sue the Navy for the loss of their boat after having been rescued by Navy helicopters. They will sometimes claim that they were never in distress, that the Navy had misidentified the distressed craft, and that if it weren't for the Navy, the Chomoran fishermen would still have a boat. In truth, the boat would have been lost with the Chomoran fishermen on board or off, but never mind that. I guess some Chomoran fishermen believe in the principle of "never let a catastrophe go to waste." New boat!

Greyhound: Somehow a former school teacher managed to finagle his way into a Marine pilot spot at the ripe old age of thirty-two. The cutoff is usually twenty-seven. So, he was sort of old for a newly winged pilot and as such was prematurely gray haired for a dude in his early thirties, but that isn't the reason he got the call sign Greyhound. While on deployment in Kuwait, his squadron was conducting interoperability training with the Kuwaiti armed forces. There is a personnel insertion/extraction technique called SPIE rigging. Using carabiners, four to six soldiers or Marines will attach themselves to a rope hanging from the bottom of a helicopter, and the helicopter will lift them safely off the ground and out of harm's way. It was developed by Marine recon units in Vietnam. On the day this CH-46 pilot earned his call sign, he was SPIE-rigging Kuwaiti soldiers . . . in the desert. You can usually stay clear of obstacles in the desert. It wasn't like there was a triple canopy of trees or anything. So our brave pilot lifted up into a hover until the rope was touching the ground with enough slack for the Kuwaiti soldiers to hook up. Once they were all hooked in, the crew chief gave the signal that it was clear to lift, and our pilot pulled in power to get enough height aboveground so he could begin forward movement. Somehow, while concentrating on taking off, he forgot what he was doing. Before he had gained sufficient height aboveground, he transitioned to forward flight and dragged the poor Kuwaiti soldiers into the side of a bus, causing several broken bones. It wasn't a Greyhound bus, but it was close enough.

THERE I WAS . . .

At the conclusion of a disaster relief mission in the Philippines, my section of CH-46Es departed Clark Air Force Base destined for Okinawa, Japan. In preparation for the entire squadron's return flight home, we had all been up late the night before, and we had all gotten up very early that morning. The flight would require nine hours of very dull flying out over the ocean blue, and fuel stops on three separate islands. Per NATOPS, we were limited to twelve hours of flight time for crew day / crew rest requirements.

So there we were at 500 feet over the cerulean waters of the Philippine Sea, with our altitude hold set to barometric pressure. Tired and weary after a night of not enough sleep, I was on the controls. The HAC was reading a book. The crew chief was looking out the gunner's window. There was a slight imbalance in the rotor blades (although well within limits) that caused a slight wobbling of the aircraft. It was similar to being in the arms of a mother who was gently rocking a baby to sleep. It didn't take long before my eyes got heavy and I started to struggle to stay awake. Usually in a situation like this, you pass the controls to the other pilot, drink some water, slap yourself in the face, and do your best to get your head straight. I was a brand-new copilot at the time, and I feared the judgment of a respected pilot such as my aircraft commander, call sign Rodeo. Clearly I was lacking some of the crew resource management skills at the time.

So, predictably, I drifted off to sleep at the controls of a CH-46, which was the lead aircraft for a section. I remember at some point I was dreaming about being in the Phrog, and somehow my brain kicked in and reminded me that I was flying a helicopter in the middle of nowhere,

The US Army came out to play naval aviators in the Philippines on USS
Wasp, and they did a pretty damn good job.

with water, water everywhere and not a drop I wanted to get on me. I came to. My eyes looked at the instruments and then to the horizon. I kept my gaze forward and pretended that I had been awake the whole time. I was deathly afraid that Rodeo had noticed. I finally sneaked a peak to my right, only to discover Rodeo with his arms crossed, chin on his chest, sound asleep. I turned to look through the tunnel and found our crew chief sacked out on the troop seats.

We were all asleep in a CH-46 flying at 120 knots, 500 feet over the Pacific Ocean. Luckily my superior flying skills (clears throat), and barometric altitude hold, had resulted in a perfectly trimmed aircraft that kept us headed in the right direction at the right speed. I woke Rodeo and the crew chief, and we did all we could to keep each other awake all the way to Okinawa. That was the longest flight of my life.

BDA: In military parlance, BDA stands for battle damage assessment. When an aircraft conducts an airstrike, for example, the crew sometimes conducts a poststrike flyby to see what damage to the enemy they accomplished. An MH-60S pilot had earned this call sign for being a Big Dumb Animal. It was applicable in more than one way, in that BDA was a bit of a clutz when he got drunk, an inebriated schleprock who left a path of destruction wherever he went, like a bull in a china shop. It was usually up to one of his squadron mates to conduct the BDA whenever BDA went out drinking.

Blunder: Back in the 1980s, there was a cartoon called *Thunder Cats*, about a bunch of cat people who fought evil with swords, magic, and magnificent hair. It was Japanese animation at its 1980s finest. I tell you that to tell you this: There was an AH-1W pilot out on a field operation who somehow managed to walk smack into a static tail rotor blade, busting his upper lip wide open. This was a stupid thing to do, so naturally it called for a call sign. His last name was Katz. Blunder Katz. Get it?

Two-Hand Dan: A Royal Air Force pilot was living the dream in San Diego on exchange with VMGR-352, a Marine KC-130J squadron. One sunny day aloft in some Military Operating Area off the coast of Southern California, Dan was flying with the squadron CO. The CO asked the intrepid Brit to execute a zoom climb. Apparently, the RAF executes these a little differently than the Marines do. For whatever reason, Dan pulled back on the yoke with both hands and neglected the power levers. In a steep climb, the speed of a bulking C-130 drops off rapidly. Luckily, and unfortunately for the crew in back, Dan recognized that he was approaching stall speed. He boldly pushed forward on the yoke to reduce the climb and build speed, without once touching the power levers. The resulting maneuver saved the plane, but due to the negative Gs, everything in the back of the aircraft that was not properly secured floated up, only to smash down on the cabin deck when the Gs caught up with the aircraft. A toolbox crashed down, resulting in tools flying everywhere. If you don't already know it, tools flying around inside an aircraft is a very bad thing. A tool could end up among control rods, resulting in a jammed control surface followed by a rapid acceleration toward the ground. Not good! Additionally, the blue water in the toilet went flying. The toilet in the back of a C-130 has no privacy. If you're gonna go, you're gonna do so in front of all who shall see these presence, greeting. The water rose from the depths of the toilet, but when it splashed down again, it went everywhere, creating a cascade of blue yuck all over the floor of the cabin. What a mess! The Brit took it all with a grain of salt, though. Two-Hand Dan is better than LOTHAR.

Cucumber: Helicopters really do it all. They can fire forward fixed aviation ordnance (say that five times fast), rescue people from precarious locations from the mountains to the sea, carry the injured to hospitals, or simply transport cargo and personnel from one place to another. There's really nothing that helicopters can't do. And of course, they can even hover. The CH-53E is the mightiest

of naval aviation helicopters. Shitter pilots often brag about their ability to lift 18,000 pounds with just one arm. These beasts of burden can lift damn near anything. Sometimes they carry equipment and cargo under their fuselage, in what is commonly referred to as a sling load. This can include cannons, vehicles, elephants, small children, you name it. In certain emergency situations, such as an engine failure, it is the aircraft commander's option to drop the underslung load, thus reducing the power load requirement on the remaining engines (the CH-53E has three engines). The term for this action is called "pickle," as in "The pilot had to pickle the load in order to save the aircraft." Pickling a load is done on purpose. If done by accident, it can be a very expensive embarrassment. The CH-53E pilot for whom this story is about accidentally dropped a Humvee into the clear blue waters off MCAS Kaneohe Bay, an event that was destined to garner a new call sign. His new call sign was Cucumber, because a cucumber is not quite a pickle.

REDNECK PARASAILING

Student naval aviators (SNAs) learn all kinds of things at Aviation Preparation Instruction before beginning flight school. The most important thing they're taught is how to fall. In the unfortunate event that a naval aviator should ever have to bail out of an unrecoverable aircraft, they'll have to know how to land when their parachute eventually brings them safely to the ground. The landing bit can be tricky, because the parachute landing is not exactly soft. So SNAs practice something called the parachute landing fall (PLF) over and over again. Hours are spent jumping from a 4-foot platform into a sand pit, practicing the proper way to fall. Keep your knees bent, and land to your strong side with your arms up to protect your neck and head. As your feet make contact with the ground, you sort of collapse like a rag doll to one side, thus dispersing the impact

Pretty in flight, ugly duckling in a hover

throughout your body. And of course, there is a final examination to test if you've mastered the ability to fall. There's a place out on the western border of Florida called Florabama. Southern college kids are familiar with Florabama because it's a popular spring break destination. Naval aviators are familiar with it because it's a great place to party on the weekends when you're in flight school. It's also where all SNAs experience the glory of redneck parasailing. Essentially, you're strapped into a harness attached to a deployed parachute. The other end of the harness is attached to a pickup truck with two good ol' boys in the cabin. At the signal "Go!," the truck begins driving across an uneven grass field, while the SNA trots behind. The trick is to run fast enough that you don't end up being dragged across the ground. Once the truck gains enough speed, at which point you're at a full sprint, the parachute blossoms full and lifts you from the ground until you're briefly flying in the air behind Cletus and Jethro. Then they stop the truck. The ground rushes up at you a lot faster than you think it should, and you suddenly remember you're supposed to do something called a PLF. You'd better get it right or you're gonna be walking funny later that night when you're partying in Florabama.

LINO: Three Cobras were flying from MCAS New River in North Carolina to fabulous 29 Palms, California, for a combined arms exercise. As they were flying through Louisiana they ran into a line of thunderstorms that impeded their progress. The squadron CO was the flight lead, and he decided to look for a hole and push through. The other two Cobras lost sight of the Old Man and decided that flying through thunderstorms was not their cup of tea. The two Cobras peeled off and diverted to New Orleans (not a bad place to divert). The weather was forecast to stay shitty well into the next evening, so they parked their Cobras at Naval Air Station New Orleans, checked into a hotel on Bourbon Street, and set in for a night of hard drinking and fraternizing with local women. As the evening wore on, the boys found themselves at a burlesque show. Somehow the four intrepid aviators got separated from each other. In the morning they discovered one of their own was MIA. They looked all over for him, to no avail. The city had him. As it turned out, the lost pilot picked up a woman at the burlesque show and she drove him out into the middle of nowhere swampland USA. They had relations, and the next day he snuck out while she was sleeping. In the middle of the night, he had somehow misplaced his beer goggles, and when he woke up he decided that it was best to let her sleep in. He had no idea where he was. The only road nearby was a dirt one, so he started walking and eventually found a paved road, hitched a ride, and made it to a good old, down-south-style gas station, where he used a pay phone to call a cab. He tried for hours before a cab company agreed to pick him up. The cabby dropped him on Bourbon Street, which was the last place he remembered being. He couldn't remember which hotel his room and all of his clothes were at, and since it was the days before cell phones, he had no way of reaching his pals. A bartender let him use the phone out back, and he started calling every hotel in the phone book asking for his buddies, with no luck. In frustration, he took another cab to the air station and decided to wait with the Cobras in the hope that someone would eventually show up. By the time they did, he had been waiting for hours in the same clothes he'd been wearing the day prior, with no shower, with bad breath, and smelling generally like crap. He'd had just about enough of New Orleans and Louisiana. LINO stands for Lost in New Orleans.

≡★≡ MAKE AIRCREW GREAT AGAIN?

Some aircrew from Helicopter Sea Combat Squadron 25 took it upon themselves to wear a shoulder patch on their flight suits that had a picture of President Donald Trump and the words

"Make Aircrew Great Again!" during Trump's Memorial Day visit to USS *Wasp* in Yokosuka, Japan, in 2019. This is why senior leadership exists. Someone failed to inspect those sailors before they reported to the hangar bay for the event, and the world took notice when CNN broke the story. In the political fallout, the Department of Defense determined that the patches were worn for humorous purposes rather than for the purposes of political affiliation, but that the patches still violated DoD Directive 1344.10. That directive prohibits service members from displaying political affiliation while in uniform. Since the patches seemed to indicate DoD affiliation to the president, the sailors and their leadership received appropriate punishment. Still, it was kind of funny. I doubt that any of the HSC-25 sailors who wore the patch, dedicated to humor at all costs or not, uttered the words "worth it!"

CNN actually wrote a decent article about the whole affair. See it here: https://www.cnn.com/2020/02/13/politics/navy-review-trump-patches/index.html.

FURBI: Some squadrons are hot messes. You get the wrong mix of people who just don't jive together, regardless of their individual merits, and you end up with a dysfunctional squadron. This was especially true for one MV-22B squadron that had just transitioned from CH-46s (God's Chariot) to MV-22s (colloquially known as plopters). The squadron pilots were a mixed bag of guys who had transitioned from other aircraft, brand-new nugget pilots straight out of the fleet replacement squadron, and a couple of majors who were the only aircraft commanders besides the CO. The CO was a wild man. None of the majors liked each other, and everyone hated the CO. The transition pilots, all former aircraft commanders in their respective aircraft, treated the nugget guys like crap. All of this made for a very hostile work environment. One nugget, a guy named Roberts, seemed to be charmed though. His first job was squadron S-5, essentially a military planner. His next job was NATOPS officer, which was pretty easy, and his job when he earned his call sign was flight equipment OIC. His fellow nuggets were working ridiculous hours planning training flights, writing schedules, and creating products for guys up for qualifications, all while trying to study, fly, and advance in the aircraft commander syllabus. Meanwhile, Roberts was going to the gym twice a day and putting beer to lips every night by 1800. As a result, he was a little behind the power curve when it came to flight planning. During a brief for a training flight that would advance him one tick closer to the aircraft commander qualification if he passed, the products he produced and his brief for the flight were well below par. In frustration, and in the midst of the hostile work environment outlined above, the instructor pilot launched into a tirade about how useless Roberts was, how he was lucky to have the jobs he'd had and not be subject to the long hours everyone else was working, and so on and so forth. The instructor finished his tirade by yelling, "F**k You, Roberts! Bitch! Idiot!!" Harsh. An onlooker in the ready room immediately recognized the acronym call sign potential and put it all together to create FURBI.

Half Ass: A UH-1N pilot had an operation that removed his large intestine and several other organs because of some severe gastrointestinal issues. It was as if this skid kid had lost half of himself. I hope it didn't also describe his work performance. This is how naval aviators do sympathy.

VI (Six): A Harrier pilot was known for being well behind the power curve in intellect, although somehow he was a decent stick. Often the cause of much unintentional laughter, he was a bit like the village idiot. They called him Six, but they didn't mean it the way the Romans did.

Pocket: In prison there's this thing called keistering. A prisoner will hide drugs, knives, revolvers, etc. up their ass in order to hide these objects from the prison guards or other prisoners. If you

remember, Christopher Walken's character in *Pulp Fiction* carried "this uncomfortable hunk of metal" up his ass while he was a prisoner in the Hanoi Hilton. In prison they call this a prison pocket when it is used for hiding an object, which brings us to our story. There was a young Marine MV-22 pilot who had entered the Navy's tobacco cessation program. Mind you, he didn't smoke, but being on the cessation program gave him free access to nicotine lozenges. Who doesn't love a free nicotine lozenge?! Anyway, the young plopter pilot was prescribed tobacco lozenges by the squadron flight surgeon, and he popped them like candy. One night in a hotel room in Sydney, Australia, the young MV-22 pilot and his buddies were significantly intoxicated. (Seems a lot of good stories start with alcohol. Some not-so-good stories too!) On a dare, our hero agreed to have a tobacco lozenge inserted into his ass to see if taking it as a suppository enhanced the effects of the nicotine. So he dropped his trousers and presented his ass to his squadron mate. With his fingers wrapped in toilet paper, the helpful squadron mate shoved the lozenge into his buddy's ass. The thing about nicotine lozenges is that they are not supposed to be taken via the anus. In fact, taking a tobacco lozenge as a suppository can straight up kill you, unbeknown to the chuckleheads in the Sydney hotel room. More disturbingly, this was unbeknown to the squadron flight surgeon too! One of the boys involved called the flight surgeon to ask if this was something that was safe to do; you know, safety first and all. The flight surgeon, unfazed apparently, told them that he couldn't imagine what could go wrong, and offered his medical blessing. After the flight surgeon hung up the phone, however, something he'd been taught in medical school, something he had long since forgotten, somehow rose to the surface and lodged itself in his frontal lobe. He decided to Google That Shit just in case. The internet doesn't lie! He frantically called the morons in the Sydney hotel room and demanded they remove the lozenge immediately. The drunk squadron mate, with his fingers still wrapped in toilet paper, attempted to remove the lozenge, but instead shoved it farther up his friend's ass. Flying down four flights of stairs, the flight surgeon arrived in the nick of time, removing the lozenge by using a pair of tweezers. He sheepishly told them that the lozenges should be taken only orally. Holding the formerly keistered lozenge up with his fingers, the man who would be known as Pocket for the rest of his life said, "I suppose I won't be taking this one orally, huh, Doc?" The short version of this story, which I received directly from the man himself, was that Pocket had used an alternate insertion/extraction method (pilot talk) for taking his lozenge. Say no more, Pocket; I got the story from someone else. Pocket is short for Prison Pocket, but you've probably already figured that out. Also, this story is an example of how ridiculous warning labels end up on product packaging.

Elton: During a training event somewhere over the Southern California desert, a young AV-8B Harrier pilot became the Rocket Man while laser-focused on his target. On his first run on the target, he was supposed to drop a 500-pound bomb at the command of a joint terminal attack controller on the ground. His second run would consist of firing 2.75-inch rockets from a wing-mounted pod. When you fire rockets, the intent is to hit the target and to do so with the smallest circular error pattern (CEP). In other words, you want all the rockets to hit in the smallest area possible to inflict the maximum amount of damage to the target. The young Harrier pilot began his attack run. He pulled into a shallow climb until he reached a point in the sky, called "the pop," where he snap-rolled the aircraft upside down, pulled the stick hard into his belly so he could visually acquire the target, and then rolled back upright, bearing down like a streak of lightning on the object of his hate and discontent. He hit the button on his controls to pickle the bomb and felt the sudden jolt as his plane shed 500 pounds of cold-rolled American steel. As the 500 pounds of cold-rolled American steel fell from his plane, our hero began his climb to go around and set up for his next attack run. Turns out, our pilot had dropped the wrong 500 pounds of cold-rolled American steel! His section leader came up on the interflight frequency and said, "Dude, you're missing a rocket pod." The young pilot accidentally hit the wrong pickle button and let loose his rocket pod filled with 2.75-inch rockets. It

tumbled harmlessly to the earth, landing near the target, but not close enough to be called a hit. Turns out that rocket pods have different aerodynamic characteristics, which screwed up his targeting solution, calculated for an aerodynamic 500-pound bomb with stabilizing fins. He could be proud of one thing, though. He had achieved the tightest CEP in the history of 2.75-inch rocket attacks. Elton John wrote a song about this slightly embarrassing story, called "Rocket Man." I guess Rocket Man was already taken, so he was named after the singer instead of the song.

G-roy: On YouTube there are thousands of videos posted of *World of Warcraft* games. WoW is a video game that some people are really, really, really into. One such video went viral for a while. In the video, all players are speaking via internet-connected headphones. One guy was the leader of a large group of *World of Warcraft* warriors, and there were a lot of video game bad guys on the other side of a door they were about to go through. The leader issued detailed orders to his fellow WoW warriors. They all agreed on the plan, when almost as an afterthought someone asked where "Leroy" was. Leroy was on the team, but he wasn't answering on his headset. His avatar just sort of did that video game bounce in the corner on the screen. It appeared he had stepped away from the game. Anyway, they opened the door and entered the room to execute their intricate plan of attack, when suddenly Leroy, out of no-where, went charging past his teammates into the thick of the bad guys. He began screaming over his headset, "LEEEEEEEEROOOOOOY JEEEEEEEENKIIIINS!!!! The end result of this was the utter annihilation of his team by the bad guys in a matter of seconds, much to the chagrin of the team leader. As you can see, there is an obvious military application to the Leroy Jenkins story. If you are a naval aviator, nay! A military pilot, nay! A member of the US armed forces, nay! A member of the military in any country, and your last name is Jenkins, your call sign, nickname, handle, etc. will invariably be "Leroy." It's like science or something. There is an exception to every rule, though. There was a Harrier pilot who earned the stupid call sign of Leroy simply because (you guessed it) his last name was Jenkins. However, Jenkins pulled a Leroy Jenkins in his jet while dropping bombs over the California desert. One of his bombing runs was a little too aggressive, and he almost pranged his jet into the ground. During the pullout of the dive, he "over-G'd" his jet, meaning he had overstressed the wings and fuse-lage. This almost led to his death, but he managed to recover and return to base. His call sign was changed immediately to G-roy, to account for his exceeding the g-limit in his plane while still main-taining the Jenkins-related call sign required by the laws of physics.

LOHO: There was a female MH-53 pilot who scared herself during a night flight (we've all been there!). She began to cry right there in the cockpit. As Tom Hanks's character so aptly said in a movie about female baseball players, "There is no crying in baseball." The other pilots felt the rule applied to naval aviation as well, and gave the poor pilot the call sign LOHO, for League of Her Own.

Ruffles: You know those chips, the ones with rrrrrridges? This is the story of a bag of Ruffles. In the naval services we have a gourmet little lunch delightfully referred to as a "box nasty," so called because it comes in a box and it's nasty. It usually consists of a meat substitute and imitation cheese slapped between a stale baguette, accompanied by a box of Minute Maid juice, packets of mustard and mayonnaise (if you're lucky), and a bag of chips. They are made for Marines and sailors who

Go already! This yellow jacket is getting inpatient for the MV-22s to get the hell off the flight deck.

Beast mode! This is a picture of the very first time the F-35B launched from a ship with a full load of external ordnance . . . I think.

don't have time to go to the chow hall or mess deck but still must be fed. Pilots are often treated to the delectable deliciousness of a box nasty when they are going to be flying through lunch or dinner. One Harrier pilot departed his ship with a box nasty in his helmet bag for a long day of flying silly circles over western Iraq, and he forgot that the box nasty came with a bag of chips. Jet cockpits are not pressurized, which is why jet pilots wear oxygen masks. As he climbed to altitude, the air pressure in the chip bag exceeded the air pressure in the cockpit, and the bag of Ruffles with rrrrrridges exploded with a loud pop. Harriers were once called "North Carolina Lawn Darts" because the A model was a fickle little airplane that had very specific flight parameters. If those parameters were pushed a little too much, it could result in the plane departing controlled flight and crashing. They've also been referred to as the Scarrier, because many a Harrier pilot has had scary close calls in the little British-designed jump jet. So it's not out of the ordinary for a Scarrier pilot to be a little jumpy when his jump jet makes a popping sound. The pilot investigated the popping sound and looked at his gauges for any secondary indications of a systems failure. He found none but decided it was better safe than sorry, and requested emergency handling to return to the ship immediately, before the Scarrier claimed another victim. As soon as he was on deck and shut down, the maintenance crews conducted a thorough investigation of the jet but were absolutely baffled by what could have caused the loud pop. There seemed to be nothing wrong, and all systems were good to go. That is, until the pilot discovered the exploded bag of Ruffles in his helmet bag. Mystery solved, but the pilot was left feeling sheepish and embarrassed. So naturally a call sign was born.

SARA: When an MH-60S pilot launches a Hellfire missile, they announce on the radio, "Actual rifle away." When doing this for training purposes, the aircrew will usually do a dry run to familiarize

themselves with the range and rehearse the procedures for launching the missile. During one such dry run, the pilot at the controls accidentally fired his Hellfire missile instead of just going through the motions. As the missile left the rail and he startlingly realized his mistake, he yelled over the radio "Shit! Actual rifle away!" (SARA).

CTAF: In the world of aviation, CTAF stands for common traffic advisory frequency. A CTAF is usually used at airports that do not have a control tower, so pilots can report their positions to other pilots in the area. So, you know, it's an aviation thing. A newly minted MH-60S copilot couldn't quite master talking on the radio while flying. The nugget MH-60S pilot Can't Talk and Fly at the same time.

NTAC: No-Talent Ass Clown. A student pilot somehow destroyed four sets of tires in one day while learning how to land an airplane.

Shroom: Be careful what you eat in the woods, kids. During SERE (Survive, Evade, Resist, Escape) school, a newly winged Navy helicopter pilot was doing all he could to survive during the survival portion of SERE school. For those of you unfamiliar with what SERE school is, it essentially trains military personnel how to survive and evade enemy capture if they ever find themselves, heaven forbid, behind enemy lines. SERE school also teaches students how to resist if captured, and how to escape. After a week of classroom instruction, students are taken out to a desolate location and dropped off, with the only instruction being to survive and evade the "enemy." The instructors then roam the countryside looking for "yankee imperialists." Once captured, the "POWs" are put into a very realistic POW camp, where they can put into practice all they learned in the classroom. The young helicopter pilot in our story was taught what he could eat to sustain energy in the wild, sort of like Bear Grylls. He was also taught what not to eat, but the lesson apparently failed to mention jimson weed, which is a pretty powerful psychedelic hallucinogen. Our hero ate a grip of it and as a result started tripping balls. He saw pretty neon lights in the sky and heard passionate tiny animal sounds in the underbrush. He wasn't the only one. Twelve other students had also "accidentally" eaten jimson weed. One was chased through the woods by a washing machine, another had a very meaningful conversation with an ex-girlfriend from high school and her father, and still another thought he was putting something away in his backpack but was horrified to find his backpack had turned into the gaping and sharp-toothed mouth of a crocodile. I don't know what happened to the other tripping students from this story, but for the newly winged Navy helicopter pilot who would be forever known as Shroom, his story reached his first fleet squadron before he did.

ARI: Alcohol is a hell of a drug. There was an F/A-18F NFO who loved to drink. He was a bit of a frat boy. His squadron was deploying the next day on a Norfolk-based aircraft carrier. He was not one of the lucky guys who got to fly onto the ship after it was underway. He boarded the ship like a run-of-the-mill sailor. This NFO went out for a bender at the officers club the night before the deployment. He drank enough to be "blind," as the Aussies say. When it was time to go back to the ship, he told his taxi driver to drop him off at the aircraft carrier. In Norfolk there are several aircraft carriers, so the taxi driver dropped him off at the first aircraft carrier he came to. The well-oiled NFO had somehow lost his military ID over the course of the evening, so when he tried to board this random aircraft carrier, he had a brief confrontation with the sailor on the quarterdeck, who refused to let him board without his ID. So the NFO improvised, adapted, and overcame. He somehow snuck passed the sailor on guard duty and got onto the ship. This being a new ship to him (especially since it wasn't his), he had no idea where his stateroom was. He decided to head to the ready room and sleep there. When he woke in the morning, he found himself in enlisted berthing, and his beloved brown flight boots had somehow gone missing. If you were a naval aviator you'd know how important those are. As he shook out the cobwebs and started piecing the night together, he noticed that something was not quite right with the ship. Something was just a little off. He suddenly realized that he was in big trouble. He was on the wrong ship. To make matters worse, the ship he was supposed to be on was pulling away from the pier in five minutes. He managed to borrow someone's shower shoes and get off the ship in a hurry. Unfortunately for him, his actual ship had already pulled up the ramp by the time he got there. The NFO begged to be let on the ship, had a verbal altercation with the command duty officer, and was finally let on when his squadron CO arrived to say, "This clown belongs to me." He's very lucky, because "missing movement" is punishable by the Uniform Code of Military Justice. The shame he carried for the entire deployment was that he was forced to wear black boots instead of the beloved brown boots worn by naval aviators. ARI stands for Alcohol-Related Incident. Aren't they all?

HYFI: A brand-new pilot showed up to an MH-60 squadron, cocky and overzealous. His very first flight in the squadron should have brought him down a notch or two, but it didn't. As they started the aircraft and prepared to taxi, the young pilot's water bottle, which he had hung from his seat back, fell from its hook, hitting the cockpit floor at an angle and spilling water everywhere. Somehow the water got into the electrical system, which immediately caused the helicopter's warning system to give indications of all kinds of malfunctions, which precluded taking off for forward flight. The blades were spinning, but the blade fold indicator indicated that the blades were folding. The HAC shut down the aircraft and walked away, shaking his head. The copilot was apparently unfazed and went on to embarrass himself in other ways from time to time. Every time he screwed up, someone would say, "Hotchkiss, You Fricking Idiot!"

NERF: The F-35B is a complicated piece of machinery. The pilot is just sort of along for the ride. The thing flies itself (F-35 pilots love when people say that). The computers are very secret-squirrel and super-wiz-bang, but sometimes they don't work as they are supposed to. F-35 pilots wear helmets that cost $600,000 apiece. That's a lot of dough! An F-35 pilot can see into the future with that thing. If it's not calibrated correctly, it can lead to some pretty embarrassing results. The pilot in our story did not see his imminent future clearly in his future-seeing helmet. While landing at MCAS Iwakuni, Japan, on a bright sunshiny day, there was something a little off with the altimeter setting that appeared on his in-helmet heads-up display. As a result he was just a little higher on the glide slope than he thought he was, which caused him to land much farther down the runway than he wanted to. Once he touched down, he had a split-second decision to make on the basis of whether or not there was enough runway or if he should put in power for a touch and go. He chose poorly. Just as he had made the decision to accept the landing, he recognized that he was too far down the runway. He did everything he could to slow his aircraft and prevent a runway overrun in an aircraft that cost a lot more than his helmet. His efforts were to no avail. He went off the end of the runway—by 2 feet. His ego was more damaged than the jet. When he got back to the ready room, his squadron mates were assembled to hear the tale. He retold the story in detail, which included him saying out loud in the cockpit, "Not Enough Runway, F**k!" But wait! There's more. NERF's call sign was subsequently changed to Shock. Here's the story: While on liberty in Brisbane, Australia, NERF tried to keep up with the Aussies and ended up having to be helped back to the Airbnb he was sharing with his squadron mates. When the rest of the jet guys returned, they found NERF curled up on the floor in the fetal position, wearing nothing but a T-shirt. As the teller of the story explained it to me, he was "Winnie the Poohing" it, with his penis hanging out below the bottom of his shirt. Shock is short for Shirt-Cock.

Byeeee! This CH-53E is headed home at the end of a deployment on board USS *Wasp*.

DET VI ARCHANGELS

THE OGs

CHAPTER 3

CHAPTER 3 SEX AND THE NAVAL AVIATOR

This chapter contains explicit material of a sexual nature. If you are younger than eighteen, **PUT THIS BOOK DOWN, YOU LITTLE PERVERT!**

In the 1980s, there was a naval flight surgeon named Capt. Frank Dully. He is considered the father of human factors / crew resource management, and he coined the phrase "failing aviator." In the 1980s, he gave a series of two fifty-five-minute presentations about sex to naval aviation crews, called "Sex and the Naval Aviator." Someone asked a thread on the internet if anyone knew where he could find copies of the video presentation of "Sex and the Naval Aviator," and these are some of the answers he received in return:

Shytorque: "Isn't this a gay movie?"
Exscribbler: "It wouldn't necessarily be a gay movie, but it would certainly be very short."
The West Coast: "Does it involve beach volleyball and arguments in the showers?"

Unfortunately, sex gets a lot of naval aviators and NFOs in trouble. The following stories are the least of the consequences that a pilot or naval aviator may face if caught in some sexual misadventure somewhere. Again, we are you and you are we, so try not to judge. None of the following stories should be particularly shocking to anyone. I will warn you now: what you are about to read you cannot unread. If you think you are about to find erotic literature here, you've definitely come to the wrong place. Will they nauseate you? Yes. Arouse you? No.

TOD: There was a Super Hornet pilot who had flown into NAS North Island in San Diego with his squadron on a cross-country from NAS Lamoore. The squadron was spending a couple of days in San Diego, and they decided to check out the scenery at Imperial Beach. TOD could throw down with the best of them when it came to drinking, and once inebriated he did not have very high standards for the women he associated with. On one particular night that I am sure will haunt him for life, he was photographed by his squadron mates at a bar in Imperial Beach making out with a biker chick who was more than qualified to wear the moniker of "cougar." His squadron mates were not entirely certain that said biker chick was actually a "chick." So TOD stands for Tongues Older Dudes.

SAS: A brand-new F-18 pilot was conducting his first training flight at his first fleet squadron. The mission was to conduct merge practice, where two F-18s would intercept each other head to head to begin a dogfight, without actually executing air combat maneuvering. The new guy was not yet qualified to conduct ACM, and the merge practice was an iterative step toward becoming a fully fledged fighter pilot. Unfortunately for the new guy, his environmental system was degraded and the temperature in his cockpit got a little too warm for comfort. While executing the tight turns and steep dives as part of the training, the new F-18 pilot began to feel a little ill, and before he could remove his oxygen mask, he blew chunks, filling his face mask with his lunch. Before he could clear the mask, he blew chunks again, but this time he managed to keep the chunks in his mouth and swallow them instead of completely filling his mask with vomit. He managed to remove his mask and pour the vomit into his helmet bag, but he felt another surge coming. This time, he puked directly into his helmet

They went thataway! A landing signals chief (you can tell because he has khaki-colored pants on) gives the signal for an F-35 pilot to release the breaks and launch from USS America.

bag, before finally calling his instructor on the radio and begging for mercy. The two F-18s returned to base, prematurely ending the training mission. When the story was brought to light at the squadron's kangaroo court, the CO asked if the new F-18 pilot had spit or swallowed his chunks, and the instructor pilot responded that the new guy had done both. SAS stands for Spits and Swallows.

TIBO: There was once an AV-8B pilot who had a little too much to drink and was enjoying himself a little too much at Yuma's favorite strip club. He spent so much money that he maxed out his credit card. He was heard in the parking lot yelling into his cell phone at his credit card company, "TURN IT BACK ON!!!"

Top Bunk: Squadron mates! Am I right?! They can sometimes behave like real douchebags. An F-18 NFO, service withheld, introduced his sister to his pilot while visiting his hometown on a cross-country flight. The pilot took a liking to this guy's sister, and she to him. After a night of drinking, one thing led to another, and the sister and pilot started going at it on the bottom bunk of a bunk bed. In the top bunk (not getting any sleep at all) was the NFO, listening to his sister and his pilot getting busy in the bed below him. Awkward!

Fife: This call sign is all about radio communication during a conversation that should have been an intercommunication system (ICS) conversation instead of a radio conversation. Let me explain. A workaround solution for a failed ICS on an aircraft is to select an arbitrary and unassigned radio frequency to talk on. If external communications work, and all on board can hear what's being said on the radio, this will allow for communication between crew members, even if ICS is down. The key is to select an unassigned radio frequency, because everything you say will go out on the airwaves. Besides the obvious need for extra operational-security awareness when using this method to communicate without an ICS, one should consider the possibility that others might be listening in on the conversation. Such was the case for an E-2C Hawkeye crew that was conducting silly circles out over the Persian Gulf one fine Navy day. Their ICS down, they selected what they thought was an unused frequency and carried on with their mission. It can get a little dull during a four-hour flight in the old Hawkeye, so to keep everyone from falling asleep, this particular crew decided to play a game of "Five." The point of the game is to answer questions, usually of an embarrassing nature, with five answers. In this case, each crew member had to name five people on the ship they would make out with. The mission commander was up first, and she started off naming her five chosen few. She managed to get all five names out before the radio crackled to life with the dreaded words "Hot mic!" Hot mic means that a station is unintentionally transmitting, and for this crew it meant that someone else who was not on board the aircraft could hear everything they were saying. Unfortunately for the mission commander on board, the arbitrary and unassigned frequency that was chosen was neither unassigned nor arbitrary. They inadvertently chose the "Helo Common" frequency, which meant that every US Navy helicopter crew in the Persian Gulf could hear the game of "Five" being played over the radio. Word got out, and by the time they landed on the ship the carrier air group commander wanted to have a word with the mission commander. There would be hell to pay! Fife is the NATO phonetic for saying the word five over the radio, since the V sound doesn't come through on staticky radio communication very well. This game of "Five" was played over the radio, and the NFO who would come to be known as Fife announced to the entire carrier air group which "fife" guys she'd make out with.

SAPR (pronounced sapper): In the military there is a person in each unit called a SAPR, which stands for sexual assault prevention response. This person advocates for service personnel who report that they were sexually assaulted. There's nothing funny about that. It's an unfortunate reality that

some people in the military are real assholes and pretend not to understand the meaning of the word "consensual." However, there is a Navy Growler pilot who has this unfortunate moniker for a call sign. Shortly after arriving home from work, he looked out his window and noticed a woman breaking into his car. He rushed outside to catch the thief, and she bolted. Still wearing his flight suit, he gave chase, finally catching up to her at a busy intersection near his home. He tried to restrain her so he could get his stuff back, but she was squirrely, and a physical altercation ensued. At one point in the scuffle, he accidentally ripped her shirt off, and she was not wearing a bra. People driving by saw this, and she started screaming that she was being sexually assaulted. The Growler pilot was just trying to get his stuff back! When the cops showed up, she told them that she was just minding her business when this lunatic came out of nowhere and attacked her. Witnesses confirmed her story, and he ended up handcuffed in the back of a police car. Luckily for him, his wife saw the police lights and rushed to his aid, letting the cops know what really happened. When the cops searched the woman, they discovered his wallet with $50 in cash and his military ID. Anyone, I think, would tell this story to their coworkers. Little did he know that his coworkers (a.k.a. squadron mates) would use this unfortunate event to give him such a churlish and mean-spirited call sign.

Video: One day before a long flight in the SAR pattern beside an aircraft carrier, an MH-60S pilot lent his external hard drive to a squadron mate so that his squadron mate could download the Hollywood blockbusters stored therein. A video was discovered in the "taxes" folder (an obvious

If you look closely at the back of the helmet of the LSE giving the signals, you can see the letters UI. UI stands for "under instruction." This sailor is going through the syllabus to become a fully qualified LHD/LHA landing signals, enlisted, and he is being closely supervised by a more senior LSE while an MV-22 hovers over the spot for a landing.

ruse) of the owner of the hard drive having sex with his girlfriend. When the owner of the hard drive returned from his long flight, he discovered several of his squadron mates jammed into his stateroom, eating popcorn and casually watching his secret video as if a matinee. "Oh, hi! Check out this movie we found!" (*Note*: I got this story from Mush, whom you can read about in "This Is the Crappiest Chapter You Will Ever Read").

Bangs: There was a naval flight officer with the last name of Guys. No joke!

NARB: Flight suits are awesome. They're cool looking and they have lots of zippers. Wearing a flight suit is like wearing a onesie, and it's super easy to get ready for work in the morning. You're essentially wearing PJs to work when you wear a flight suit. They do have a slight downside, which is reminiscent of awkward middle-school days. A Navy EA-6B pilot was giving a safety brief to his squadron mates in the ready room when, for no apparent reason, a slight bulge started to grow in his groinal area. He awkwardly made quick adjustments to his flight suit to try to hide his growing concern as he continued on with his presentation, but the bulge continued to grow until it was readily apparent to everyone in the room that he had a raging erection. Imagine a tent pole under a tent. Flight suits may be cool green PJs with lots of zippers, but they aren't very good at hiding a boner, as I am sure every man who has ever worn one can attest. We've all been there, just not as publicly as this poor Prowler pilot who was standing tall in more ways than one. You see, sometimes men get erections for no reason at all. When this happens, it's called a No-Apparent-Reason Boner.

Manty: There is very little privacy on the boat. Although I am told that privacy can be found in the fan rooms, for those of you who are looking. And you know, being on a ship can be lonely sometimes. Thousands of miles away from home on a boat filled mostly with dudes can really make a guy miss the kind of physical attention he's used to getting from his significant other. Sometimes dudes take matters into their own hands (so to speak). The problem one faces, however, is that generally a junior officer shares a room with three other guys, so finding a secluded spot to "treat yo self" can be a challenge, as the E-2 Hawkeye pilot in our story unfortunately came to discover. His wife had thoughtfully sent him a care package, which included a pair of her panties. He indulged himself by wearing the panties over his head while enjoying a little "me time" alone in his stateroom. Unfortunately for him, his roomies walked in and caught him red handed (so to speak). He was a MAN with PANTIES on his head while spanking the monkey, so . . . Manty.

BITO (Beeto): Have you ever seen the movie *Seven*? (Spoiler alert) Do you remember that scene at the end when Brad Pitt's character is freaking out because he KNOWS what's in the box? "What's in the box? What's in the box?" A young AV-8B pilot had a similar experience one day out at sea on USS *Essex*. His girlfriend sent him a USPS box with another box inside. The box inside was pink and wrapped with a pretty pink bow. Our boy was convinced she was sending him this care package to announce that he was about to be a dad. He wasn't ready to be a dad, especially considering the fact that he and his girlfriend were unmarried. What would his parents say? He immediately launched into panic mode. "What's in the box? What's in the box?" Unfortunately for him, he opened his care package in the ready room among his squadron mates, who all gleefully watched the meltdown unfold. There was a happy ending for the young Harrier pilot, though. It was just a care package that his girlfriend had thoughtfully wrapped with a pink bow to make it look nice. She was not pregnant after all, but the unwarranted meltdown earned him a new call sign. BITO stands for Bun in the Oven.

An LSE signals the crew of a CH-53E to slide left and take off from USS *Wasp* off the coast of Subic Bay in the Philippines.

Simba: This is not the last time that *The Lion King* will be referenced in this book. A Navy F-14 pilot was having sex with his wife, as one does. As his climax approached, he asked the love of his life if he could finish on her breasts, which of course she agreed to. After the deed was done, the two love-birds were lying in bed shoulder to shoulder, basking in the afterglow, when the F-14 pilot's wife had a funny little idea enter her pretty head. "Should I?" she thought to herself. Without waiting for an answer from her internal self, the F-14 pilot's wife swiped some of her husband's spoo from her chest with her thumb and wiped it across her husband's forehead as she reverently said, "Ssssssimmba!" Why he shared this story with his squadron mates is a real head-scratcher.

COUNT: Long-distance relationships are challenging, especially for a P-3 NFO whose girlfriend lived in the US while he was stationed in Japan. Before I get into this story, the guy who shared it with me emphasized that it was important to note that this guy was a little weird. He was probably a goth in high school, and way too into *World of Warcraft*. So "count" by itself is reflective of his creepy person-ality. The girlfriend asked her faraway boyfriend if he would be willing to pay for her to get a breast augmentation. He initially refused, but when she said that her dad would pay for half, he relented. Weird dad, right?! So he paid a hefty sum to help pay for his girlfriend's new knockers, and she subsequently dumped him for another guy. Once again, someone shared way too much with their squadron mates. The original call sign they came up with was Co-owner of Unseen New Tits. As you can see, there isn't a lot of sympathy in a squadron. The story does not end there. Eventually, his ex-girlfriend realized the error of her ways and came to the conclusion that any man willing to go halfsies with her dad on her new boobies was good enough to keep around. Once they were back together, the acronym changed slightly to Co-owner of Used New Tits. The only thing about this call sign story that has me scratching my head is why a dad would pay half the bill for his daughter's breast augmentation. Weird!

SEVEN: An F-18 pilot met a Navy nurse at a bar and was trying to get her into bed. She was not one to fall into bed with someone she met on the first night, so the F-18 pilot played it cool. They spoke for a couple of hours over drinks, and during the conversation the nurse mentioned that her brother was severely crippled both mentally and physically and was confined to a wheelchair. When she found out that her new bar friend was a Navy F-18 pilot, her eyes lit up, because her brother loved airplanes. He kindly offered to show her brother around the squadron and take him out to see the jets on the flight line the following Monday. The Navy nurse showed up on Monday pushing her brother along, and the Navy F-18 pilot took them on a grand tour of the squadron spaces and the flight line. He made the poor kid's day. Later that night, after dinner and drinks, the Navy F-18 pilot took the Navy nurse to bed. She must have been very impressed by the gesture, but it was all just a trick to get her in the sack. SEVEN stands for Shamelessly Exploited a Vegetable in Exchange for a Nurse. Geez! This one is terrible! Oh stop! They eventually got married, so it's not all bad!

✈ PROWLER STORY

The squadron that possessed the pilot known as FUPA had some characters in it. Their operations officer had the call sign Good Deal because he was always trying to sell not-so-good deals as really good deals. When the squadron deployed to Afghanistan, they chose the call sign "Good Deal," to identify their squadron while conducting missions. Their aircraft were assigned 6-1 through 6-9 as their mission numbers. Good Deal 6-9 (usually pronounced as six nine in pilot speak) was always the aircraft held in reserve to support high-priority special-operations missions. The aircrew flying Good Deal 6-9 loved showing up and telling the JTAC on the ground, "Good Deal Sixty-Nine checking in!"

Skittles: Two Marine CH-53 pilots attended a party. One of the 53 pilots met a young lady who, after a flirty conversation, casually asked him if he would like to receive oral pleasure. The two snuck off to an empty room, and the 53 pilot did receive what was offered. She was not interested in taking it any further, and the two went their separate ways. Later that night, the satisfied 53 pilot found his buddy making out with the same woman who had earlier given him head. The 53 pilot who was making out with the woman received more than just mouth herpes. He also got a new call sign. The 53 pilot who had been orally pleasured had the call sign Rainbow. Do you remember the catch phrase for the fruity candy called Skittles? Give it a minute.

Tosser: Two F-35s returning to Yuma from dropping bombs in California lined up for the break turn, with the dash-two F-35 flying in parade formation (tucked in close to lead's wing). As briefed before the flight, the CO, who was in the lead aircraft, would conduct his break turn and the dash-two pilot would count four seconds before conducting his break turn. This way the two jets would gain lateral separation. Our hero forgot this important bit of information, and he stayed right on the CO's wing throughout the break turn, and most of the downwind leg. The CO had no idea dash-two was still flying in parade formation, expecting his young dash-two pilot to gain separation with the four-second count at the break. Dash-two realized his mistake at the last minute and slowed his jet, gaining 1,000 feet of separation as the CO's wheels touched down on the runway. Tower called out the situation to the CO, recommending that he keep the speed of his rollout up because his dash-two was fast approaching the runway and would likely crash right up the tailpipe of the CO's jet. The CO put in power and kept rolling down the runway until he had actually rolled onto the runway overrun. He'd been run off the runway by the wannabe Blue Angel. The dash-two made a safe enough landing, and both aircraft re-turned safely to their flight line. Tosser was earned because like a prison salad tosser, he was right up the CO's rear end on that landing. If you don't know what salad tossing is in prison, it's best that you don't find out. However, feel free to Google salad tossing with the following two notes, warnings, and cautions: Googling salad tossing is NSFW, and once you see it you cannot unsee it.

Merkin: A Marine F-18 squadron was in Kansas City for an exercise with the Royal Air Force. The exercise successfully completed, the junior officers in the squadron were celebrating the way Marine pilots do. They were all drunk as skunks in a hotel room, and they were out of adult beverages. One of them came up with the great idea of stripping down to underwear, taking over the squadron CO's room, and drinking his booze. At 3:00 a.m. they stumbled to the CO's room and pounded on the door. When he opened it, they bum-rushed him. The party ensued, and the CO's booze stash was raided. Shenanigans were unleashed. One young F-18 pilot was standing on the CO's bed and drink-ing a bottle of Jack Daniels when one of his squadron mates attempted to pants him. He failed and did so miserably. Instead, he completely ripped the underwear away from the elastic band except for a small flap of fabric that hung over the victim's butt crack. Undeterred, the young F-18 pilot, now mostly naked, continued drinking from the bottle. The CO was displeased and insisted that the mostly naked pilot cover himself. Thinking on his feet, the mostly naked pilot brought the flap of fabric around to the front to cover his rod and tackle, but the fabric wasn't long enough. Someone suggested he put on a merkin. Before I heard this story, I was unaware that merkin was a thing. The porn industry uses pubic wigs, called merkins, for reasons I can't begin to imagine, nor do I want to. Anyway, a call sign was born, and one of America's "best of the best" is named after the porn industry term for pubic wig. Also, I recently found out that merkins were invented during the Renaissance. Hygiene was a bit lacking in French courts, and as such lice was a huge problem for everyone, including royalty. To avoid lice, members of the nobility would completely shave off all of their hair, from their heads to their toes. They wore elaborate wigs to cover up their self-imposed baldness, and before sleeping with someone they would apply a merkin to hide the fact that they

Right here, dude!

had shaved off their pubes. That has absolutely nothing to do with this story, call signs, or naval aviation, but there you go.

Shady: Everyone seems to know that one guy who is just kind of creepy (maybe you are that one guy!). Either way, no one is gonna leave their kids with this creep. There was an MH-60R pilot who was known for being a total creeper whenever he went to bars and clubs, and his persona and personal appearance screamed, "Hide your wife and kids!" He even had a "molestache," which completed the predatory look. Unfortunately for him, his last name was Lerkure.

Sexo: In a CH-53E squadron stationed in Hawaii, there was once a bald mustachioed Big Iron pilot whose appearance gave him sort of a pervy look. It was his shaved head and his wispy and poorly executed mustache that accentuated his pedo persona. Adding to the problem of his appearance was the fact that his last name was the same as the famous electric guitar maker—you know the one, right? His last name was Fender. "Sexo" Fender! It must have taken a real genius to come up with that one.

Red: While attending one of those shows in Pattaya, Thailand, where Thai women demonstrate the dexterity of their biology by shooting darts or ping-pong balls with a simple Kegel maneuver, or some such talent, a young CH-53E pilot volunteered to assist in a performance when a beautiful Thai woman mounted the stage. He had no idea what he was getting himself into. Her particular talent was for sticking things where the sun doesn't shine, but he didn't know this. His squadron mates knew, but he was in the dark (so to speak). She sat him down on a stool and placed one of his feet on a slightly shorter stool. Then she removed his shoe and sock before covering his entire foot in personal lubricant. His squadron mates were giggling like schoolgirls, cheering him on. The young CH-53E pilot was pretty drunk by this point, so he wasn't really catching on to what was about to

A senior LSE walks the walk on USS *Wasp*.

happen. Before he could say anything, the beautiful Thai woman sat down on his foot and it disappeared completely. Not just the toes, but the whole foot, all the way down to the heel. *That '70s Show* had a character named Red Forman. He was the no-nonsense dad, with old-school values and little patience for BS. His favorite saying was "I'll stick a foot in your ass!" If the shoe fits . . .

Spud: Here's another call sign story earned in Thailand. There was once a Marine C-130 pilot who was deployed to Utapao, Thailand, for Exercise Cobra Gold. While on liberty one night, he and his squadron mates wandered into a club where Thai women, like the one mentioned in the above call sign story, exhibited their unique talents. They could pull a string of razor blades from their womanly parts without cutting themselves and pop balloons with darts like a South American native with a blow gun chasing Indiana Jones. These women could give you heads or tails with a roll of coins if you asked them to. One woman had a particular talent for shooting small red potatoes across the room. The C-130 pilot who would become Spud had a couple too many drinks and probably would have made a better decision had he been more sober. Unfortunately for him and fortunately for us, decisions were made. As the Thai woman shot a potato across the room, the C-130 pilot harnessed the power of his inner ninja and snatched the potato from the sky. He could barely walk back to his hotel, but somehow he caught this little red flying object in a low-lit room with lots of flashing lights. I guess he got lucky? What he did next would make him legendary in a sick and twisted sort of way. He put the potato in his mouth, chewed while savoring the flavor, and then swallowed. I'm pretty sure he caught a scorching case of ghana-sypha-herpilese.

⬲⭐⬱ FUN FACT

Tinder is a relatively new app that allows you to meet women or men online so that you can arrange a time and place to meet for coffee, read poetry, and take a walk in the park while discussing existentialism. Okay, we all know what Tinder is used for. When USS *Wasp* pulled into Sydney Harbor for a port visit in the winter month of June, Tinder use increased in the city of Sydney by 800 percent. The *Daily Telegraph*, a Sydney newspaper, ran a full front-page news story that showed the blurred-out face of a US sailor standing in front of *Wasp* (which was his Tinder profile picture), and the headline for this story read "Stars and Swipes" (pretty cheeky, Sydney). The article referred to the uptick in Tinder usage as the Tinder Blitz and Tinder Surge brought to Sydney by the arrival of USS *Wasp*.

Snitch: Back in the old debauched days of naval aviation, there were some naval aviators who partook of the delights of the night in places such as Thailand and the Philippines. A young Marine Phrog pilot deployed with his squadron to the Philippines for an exercise. He observed that some of the pilots in his squadron, who happened to be married, picked up bar girls and took them to their rooms. The young Marine captain's faith in God was strong, and he was very upset with his fellow pilots who cheated on their wives. Returning to home station, the young captain decided that he would tell his wife about how bad some of the other pilots had been and how he had been a good boy. In turn, his wife told the other wives about what their husbands had been up to. So the captain earned the call sign Snitch. A couple of years later he was the operations officer of his old squadron. In the course of a year he managed to clip three trees with his rotor blades, one such incident occurring in Yuma, Arizona, where trees are scarce, you know, in the desert. Many call sign suggestions were put forth in the call sign suggestion log located in the squadron ready room. Some of the suggestions included "Tree Killer," "Clipper," and "Gardner," to name a few. The junior officers got wise to what was going on and believed that perhaps "Snitch" was

purposely chopping trees down with his rotor blades in order to change his call sign. It was well known that he did not like his call sign, but he was stuck with it until it was changed by the ruling of the squadron CO at a kangaroo court. The junior officers replaced all the suggested call signs with variations of the word "snitch." Snitchy-poo, Snitchums, and Snitcherino come to mind. When it came time for the kangaroo court, the squadron voted overwhelmingly to preserve the call sign "Snitch" for the operations officer. He's retired now, and he still hates that call sign.

Soup Kitchen: The bearer of this call sign told me that he received his call sign because he drove a Toyota Prius. Some of you have instantly put the pieces together and figured out that soup kitchen is slang for homeless people breaking into your car for the purpose of having sex. I did not know this when I heard this call sign, because I had not yet seen the movie *The Other Guys*. Instead, I was told that the call sign "Soup Kitchen" was a lame reference to liberals who drive Toyota Priuses and volunteer at actual soup kitchens. Lies and deceit, lies and deceit, lies and deceit! He received his call sign because of the scene in *The Other Guys* when the homeless guys have a homeless orgy in the back of a Prius. I'm on to you, Soup Kitchen!

Gizzard: People keep strange pictures on their smartphones. For instance, the son of a plastic surgeon had a picture of his older sister's vagina taken prior to her vaginal rejuvenation operation. He also had the postoperative picture, but this call sign is not about his sister's rejuvenated lady bits. Why did he have a picture of his older sister's lifeless vagina, you ask? His father began letting his son scrub in to operations when he was a young teenager. He assisted with his mother's breast augmentation, his younger sister's breast reduction, and of course his older sister's vaginal rejuvenation operation. All of these he documented on his smartphone, supposedly for science. Of course, he didn't grow up to be a plastic surgeon; he grew up to be a Marine Harrier pilot. He still scrubbed in with his dad from time to time, which is why he had the very recent photos of his sister's anatomical features. All of this was completely normal to him, so much so that he couldn't conceive that showing these pictures to his squadron mates might raise an eyebrow or two. Which brings us back to his sister's preoperative vagina photo. In the photo her vagina looked like turkey gizzards, and this may be the strangest way that a pilot has received a call sign in the sordid history of call signs.

⬛⭐⬛ PIGS IN SPACE

The Muppets have a bit where Miss Piggy and her fellow piggy pals are space travelers traveling through the cosmos on intergalactic and hilarious adventures. In El Centro, California, there is a naval air station that is host to all kinds of naval aviation training. The Blue Angels, for instance, spend the off-season in El Centro, honing their skills for the upcoming air show season. Young naval aviators going through the fleet replacement squadrons will often conduct their first-ever night flights while wearing night vision goggles (NVGs) there. The surrounding area in El Centro is flat, desert and patchwork farmland. The scenery is a bit dull, but when you fly around over the El Centro training area on NVGs, you feel like you're flying around the Sea of Tranquility on the surface of the moon. When you're not flying in El Centro, there isn't much to do for nightlife activities. On base there is an All Hands club, and on Friday and Saturday nights the locals are invited on base to mix it up with young pilots, NFOs, enlisted maintenance crews, and a mixed bag of other military and contract personnel. The men outnumber the women six to one, and the women are the most attractive that the El Centro flats have to offer. Most of them are pushing 200 or even 300 pounds. The All Hands club has been dubbed "Pigs in Space," as a result of the oversized female clientele and the moonlike surroundings. Not very PC, I know.

LSEs are the bread and butter of flight deck operations. They keep everyone safe and are always looking around, their heads constantly on a swivel. One misstep and some- one can get killed or injured, and there is little room for error. They do a hell of a job!

Hold up!

YATO and **WISP**: Two students in flight school met and fell in love. Both became Marine jet pilots and married each other in holy matrimony. The wife was selected to be the first-ever female Marine F-35B pilot. The husband was assigned to fly the legacy F-18. On the F-35B, there is a system that tells the pilot if a missile that has been fired by the enemy is directed at their airplane. YATO literally stands for You Are the One. When your YATO horn sounds, you'd better do some of that pilot shit or you're going to have a very bad day. Of course, YATO received her call sign because she was the chosen one, selected from on high by the gods of Marine aviation to be the first-ever female Marine F-35B pilot. You better believe it! And Marine Corps propaganda exploited the hell out of her momentous and well-earned achievement. She was chosen by the commandant himself as the recruitment poster child for other young women to follow their dreams and become Marine pilots. Her husband, being the lowly F-18 pilot that he was, clearly did not have the piloting skills required to fly the most advanced fighter in the world. You see, his Wife Is the Superior Pilot.

Jenna: It's never a good idea to film yourself having sex. It wasn't a good idea before social media and portable devices, and it's especially not a good idea in today's world. This is the story of a viral video that should not have gone viral. A CH-53E crew was listening to music via an iPod that had been jury-rigged so the crew could listen to the music on the intercommunication system during a routine mission in western Iraq. The iPod belonged to the aircraft commander, who was a young and fairly attractive woman. The crew chief so enjoyed the aircraft commander's music selection that he asked if he could borrow her iPod so he could get the music off the device for his own music library. She handed over the iPod . . . and that was when she messed up. The crew chief, while exploring the iPod's contents, discovered a sex video of the hot female CH-53 pilot and some dude. The crew chief naturally shared this video with his fellow CH-53E crew chiefs, who naturally shared it with their CH-46 crew chief pals, and from there the video literally spread like wildfire all over Iraq wherever Marine combat units resided. Turns out the dude in the video was a Marine F-18 pilot who was deployed to Iraq with his squadron, and as a result of the video, he earned the call sign Jenna, as in Jenna Jameson the famous adult film star.

MACHO: If you marry a stripper, it may not go as well as you think it will. Sure, she's hot, she knows how to party, and her skin is so soft and bronzy. However, there may be some baggage there that led her to dancing naked for drunk and horny men that you didn't see through all of the stripper glitter. There's an infamous "gentlemen's" club in Yuma called Platinum. It's a very original name for a strip club. A young Harrier pilot fell head over heels for a stripper called Candy, or Chastity, or Harmony, or Innocence, or some such name. Turns out she was a crazy woman. Certifiably insane. No, she was totally bonkers. She dabbled in smoking meth, liked to cut herself, and really enjoyed spending all of the young aviator's money on clothes, shoes, and of course meth. She also dabbled in hitting him and trying to scratch his eyes out. Not cool. So he did what any sane Harrier pilot who married a bat-guano-crazy stripper would do, and got the marriage annulled. She was sent packing back to Platinum. He is a marine, and he dates (sometimes marries) strippers, and he's a Harrier driver. Pretty macho dude, right? Nope. MACHO . . . Married a Crazy Ho.

GUTTS: There is an MH-60S pilot whose last name starts with a G. He is of Hispanic descent, although his Ancestry.com DNA test indicates he's descended from people all over the globe. This guy was my roommate on "the boat." I assumed GUTTS was short for his last name. I was wrong. When he was a junior officer stationed in Fallon, Nevada, he and his fellow JOs took a road trip to Reno for a night on the town. Not surprisingly, they ended up at a Reno strip club, where my future roomy proceeded to get sloshy, blackout drunk. He offered his credit card up to the strip club gods as tribute and ran up an astronomical bill, paying out tips to all of his favorite strippers. Apparently they were

ALL his favorite strippers. Not only that, but he was buying dances for his pals left and right. His credit card bill came out to $3,200. So GUTTS is an acronym for Gives Unlimited Tips to Strippers. I am pretty sure his picture is on the wall at that strip club in Reno, where he is still spoken of today in reverent whispers. His wife hates his call sign. He seems okay with it.

Vespa: An E-2D Hawkeye pilot had a penchant for large women. Dating a large woman is all fun and all until someone sees you doing it, sort of like riding a Vespa scooter.

Gurglar and **Flipper**: Now pay attention. This story has some plot twists and turns, and it involves a love triangle. A skid kid was dating a local woman. It didn't last. She left him and started dating another skid kid from the same squadron. Here's the plot twist: the Johnny-come-lately skid kid was a woman. So the lady skid kid who was dating the woman who used to date her squadron mate got the call sign "Gurglar," which stood for Girl Burglar. The guy who got dumped and left out of the love triangle got the call sign "Flipper," because he was such a terrible boyfriend that he "flipped" his ex-girlfriend into dating chicks! This call sign story is a twofer!

Trunchbull: The following story was relayed to me by a Cobra pilot, call sign Donny. You'll read more about Donny later.

The setting: At an air-ground integration exercise in the desert outside Yuma, Arizona, there was an observation point set up on a place called OP Iris Wash. A section of badass (Donny's words, not mine) AH-1W Super Cobras thumped through the sky, and the radio at the OP crackled to life. It was somewhere above 115 degrees, and the tired Devil Dogs were wearing their full battle rattle. Set up in the OP, they had a pristine view of the target area.

The conversation:

(Female Cobra pilot [radio]) "Trinity Air, Trinity Air, this is Scarface 1-1 checking in as fragged from the south at angels two."

(Donny [radio]) "Scarface 1-1, this is Trinity 8-7, roger up as fragged, say playtime and proceed direct HA Sally. No other traffic on station."

(Arty FO [speaking]) "Donny, who is that flying? She has one of the sexiest voices I have ever heard."

(Donny [speaking]) "Brother, let me tell you about that one. You won't think she's so . . . se—" [interrupted by radio]

(Female Cobra pilot [radio]) "Scarface 1-1 proceeding to HA Sally at Angels two, ready for game plan and 9-line."

(Donny [radio]) "Scarface 1-1, standby on game plan and 9-line. Report when established."

(Donny [speaking]) "Dude, seriously she isn't that . . ." [interrupted by Arty FO]

(Arty FO [speaking]) "Don't take this away from me. I don't want to know anything about her except for her call sign."

(Donny [radio]) "Scarface 1-1, confirm TPL and OAD version 2.1 on board."

(Female Cobra pilot [radio]) "Trinity 8-7, affirm, both on board."

(Donny [radio]) "Scarface 1-1, copy, catalog targets in TAI two. Report back in 10 mikes or with TPL priority three or higher."

(Female Cobra pilot [radio]) " Scarface 1-1 wilco."

(Arty FO [speaking]) "Serious, just her call sign."

(Donny [speaking]) "Dude, she is brand new; no call sign yet."

(Arty FO [speaking]) "I'll call her princess. She could be my princess."

(Donny [speaking]) "All right, man. If that's what you want."

Backstory: The female Cobra pilot nicknamed by the Arty forward observer as "Princess" did eventually earn a call sign. The call sign she was given reflects not only her physical prowess as a softball player, but also her physique and demeanor in general. The call sign bestowed was "Trunchbull," after the character in the major motion picture *Matilda*. Thirty-plus days in the desert can make a man want to think of any sweet voice as belonging to some goddess. This was no exception, and had the Arty FO and "Princess" ever met, he would likely have stopped calling her Princess. She'd probably have broken his nose if he had called her that.

Astro: A young Navy lieutenant junior grade had just checked in to his MH-60S squadron on the East Coast. He was serving his time as the operations duty officer (ODO) in the ready room when a bag of burritos was delivered for some of the pilots in the squadron. Assuming one of the burritos was for him, the ODO had taken a couple of bites out of one when a squadron mate pointed out that the burrito he was eating was meant for the squadron CO. Later that same day, the ODO was in the Navy Exchange when a middle-aged woman noticed his squadron patch and said hi to him. He returned the courtesy, and the two entered into light conversation. The woman mentioned that she was a marathon runner and was looking for a product called Glide that prevented nipples from chafing during long runs. She asked the young pilot if he knew where she could find this product. The young pilot was confused. The only product with the word "glide" in it that he knew of was a personal lubricant for intimate situations. So he sought clarification. "Do you mean AstroGlide?" he said. A bit shocked, the woman said that was not what she meant. She had a good laugh. Unbeknown to him, the woman was his new squadron CO's wife. As a result of this chain of events, the young pilot earned the call sign "Nibbles," which somehow was a cross between the two stories. But in the mind of his new shipmates, when he reported aboard USS *Wasp* as the Micro Boss, the call sign did not fit the story. I began an aggressive campaign to change his call sign to Astro, because it was funnier than Nibbles and made more sense when applied to the story of his chance encounter with his new CO's wife. I could have suggested Lube. Unfortunately, my efforts were thwarted when a commander made a decision that it would remain Nibbles because some people were calling him Nibbles and some people were calling him Astro, which created confusion in a profession that does not tolerate confusion. Alas. You'll always be Astro to me, Tim!

Ball-Gag: There are guys out there whose call signs are Mumbles because they mumble everything. Other guys are called Marbles because either they've lost theirs or they talk as though their mouths are stuffed with them. Ball-Gag was one that I had never heard before. Have you ever seen the scene in *Pulp Fiction* where Marcellus Wallace and Butch are strapped to chairs in the sex dungeon of some real creepos, and they are both wearing ball gags? In that scene Wallace is protesting his treatment, desperately trying to express himself verbally while his mouth is stuffed with a red ball gag. There was a Navy C-130 pilot who could not be understood to save his life. The way he talked wasn't quite mumbling or simply some strange speech impediment. It was more like he was desperately trying to get words out but an invisible ball gag prevented him from saying what he so desperately wanted to say.

Raw Dawg: If you don't know what raw dawging is, you can GTS. There is an MV-22B pilot out there somewhere who has ten kids.

SEEK MEDICAL ATTENTION

All naval aviators abide by the Naval Aviation Training, Operations, and Procedures Standardization (NATOPS) manual for their particular aircraft. Each aircraft has its own NATOPS, and as a young pilot learning how to fly your aircraft, you become very familiar with reading it until you want to poke your eyes out with a lead pencil. Since it comes with a fabulous blue cover, it is colloquially known as the large blue sleeping pill. It's a dry read and it will put you to sleep. NATOPS manuals don't write themselves. As the saying goes, they are often written in blood. Someone somewhere did something stupid in the aircraft, causing death, injury, or loss of an aircraft, and, in so doing, wrote another rule, procedure, or regulation in the NATOPS. Amendments to the NATOPS are made by aviators from across the fleet at NATOPS conferences to make changes and promulgate those changes so that all may avoid the mistakes of others. The convention attendees, being naval aviators, sometimes bring some tomfoolery to the proceedings. At an SH-60B NATOPS conference, there was some discussion about a system called RAST, which is just a cable that is attached to the bottom of the SH-60B, and the other end is attached to the flight deck of a small ship. This is used when the weather and seas are rough and there is a need to assist the pilot in landing the helicopter on a bobbing and weaving flight deck. The system literally reels the helicopter in once the cable is attached to its underside. The cable is attached to the RAST probe on the bottom of the aircraft, which the pilot extends with the flip of a switch, so the deck crewman can attach the cable. During the NATOPS conference, the guy typing up the changes to the SH-60B NATOPS stepped away from his desk and made the mistake of leaving his computer screen unlocked. Some clown managed to type the following as a warning note in the draft copy of the amended NATOPS: "If RAST probe is extended for more than four hours, seek medical attention." As you might suspect, this is a play on Viagra's warning label. As you know, Viagra is the miracle male enhancement drug. The culprit hit save and then walked away. No one was the wiser until it was actually published. It somehow survived subsequent NATOPS conventions, because it stayed in the SH-60B NATOPS manual for over a decade.

Pissed-OL (pronounced Pistol): A Navy MH-53 pilot who was on deployment in Lithuania went out for some drinks with his squadron mates. A beautiful Lithuanian woman in a bar they stopped in for a few too many took a liking to him, and he to her. There was one tiny little problem; he was married. Temptation is a powerful motivator, and when it was pretty clear that she wanted to take him home, he was too weak to resist her. On the way back to her place, he had a stroke of conscience and began to question his actions. She still managed to get him up to her apartment, and before long she was topless and sitting in his lap, kissing and sucking on his face and neck. He knew this was wrong and that he shouldn't stray from his devoted wife. He began to protest vehemently, but she was very insistent. He didn't know what he should do to break contact. The good news is that he was pretty well sauced. Alcohol can be a solution to your problems after all. In a desperate act to save his marriage, the young MH-53 pilot pissed himself while the beautiful Lithuanian temptress was busy trying to get her freak on. She was not impressed and immediately insisted that he leave, which he was only too happy to do. A marriage was saved. He returned to the bar he had left only moments before and explained to his squadron mates why he had urinated all over himself. You see, he Pissed on Own Leg to save his marriage.

HIV: Yes, this CH-53E pilot is called HIV. However, it's pronounced Hi-Five. Five is simply replaced by the Roman numeral V, so that it looks like HIV when it is written out, such as on his leather name tag he wears on his flight suit. This mild-mannered family man and hard-charging Marine officer had

Take a picture; it'll last longer. Ordnance men like to say IYAOYAS, if You Ain't Ordnance, You Ain't Shit.

Changing of the guard. Crash crew getting ready to swap out for night ops.

So bored with this shit. One of the world's premier stealth fighters launches from the deck a mere 12 feet from where they sit, but it's just another hot, miserable day at the office for this crash-fire-rescue crew.

a sordid past. He was married rather late into his Marine Corps career, having ten years to roam the countryside looking for women to consort with as a young and single naval aviator. He was handsome and charming and was very good at convincing women to go to bed with him. He was prolific. For ten years he was a total slut. His squadron mates started to feel concerned about their young, likable fellow pilot, so when it came time to assign him a call sign, they decided to give him something that would serve as a warning to women. He needed something that would convince him to correct the error of his ways, perhaps even something that would scare women away so that he might be saved from himself. So the call sign is pronounced the way it is, but it means what it means. No, he does not have HIV, but he surely would have been "bitten by the green monkey" if he had carried on. It should be noted that his new bride, who was not aware of the spelling of his call sign, was a bit shocked to learn that her wonderful new husband was named after the human immunodeficiency virus.

Machine: A very mild-mannered F-35B pilot who weighed about 145 pounds soaking wet was out with his squadron mates to celebrate the conclusion of an Air Force Tac Air training exercise in Kansas. There were many drinks in tiny glasses consumed. Machine was approached by one of the local barflies, and the two hit it off. His new friend outweighed him by at least 145 pounds, but that did not stop mild-mannered Machine from going home with this girthful woman. The conclusion that his fellow squadron mates came to was that if Machine was able to satisfy a woman twice his size, he must be pretty well endowed for such a small guy. In their inebriated imaginations, Machine's penis took on legendary proportions. Machine's full call sign is Fat D**k Frank the Sex Machine, but you can't paint that on the side of an aircraft.

LATCH: Common sense would usually prevent a young captain from doing anything untoward to the wing's commanding general's girlfriend at a reception in front of all to see. A Harrier pilot who was three sheets to the wind took a liking to the general's girlfriend. He walked straight up to her and smacked her on the ass, right in front of his CG, colonels, his squadron commander, and his squadron mates. He somehow survived the encounter and earned a call sign for this infamous act. Likes Ass of the CG's Honey.

The Grapes are ready for action. Without the Purple Shirts, no one flies because you can't get very far without fuel.

Milkman: Ah, Thailand. Many call signs have been born there in the land of smiles. A Cobra pilot was enjoying a night out in Pattaya with his fellow skid kids when they stumbled into a ping-pong show, a common tourist attraction in Thailand. Don't Google ping-pong shows. Our Cobra pilot, who was drunk, was throwing ping-pong balls back at one woman while laughing hysterically. She responded by squirting the obnoxious Cobra guy in the face with her breast milk. The laugh, and the milk, was on him. He stopped throwing ping-pong balls at her after that.

NMRD (pronounced Nimrod): A UH-1N pilot had a squad of kids. He was an Irish American ginger, white as the driven snow. His wife was a Latina, with long dark-brown hair, brown eyes, and skin dark and smooth. Their kids all looked like her: dark-brown hair, brown eyes, and skin that matched their mother's. There was not an Irish freckle to be seen on any of those children. This Huey pilot's squadron mates became convinced that these children were the spawn of a Mexican mailman, and not that of the ginger. The call sign NMRD was given as a prediction of the realization that his children would eventually come to: this man is Not My Real Dad.

Carlos: Marines love history. In Vietnam there was a Marine sniper named Carlos Hathcock who had killed so many of the enemy that he became the highest-ranking Marine sniper in history. He was credited with ninety-three confirmed enemy kills but was estimated to have killed as many as 400. His mantra was "one shot, one kill," and it became the motto of the Marine Corps marksmanship program. There was a Marine CH-53D pilot who married his sweetheart. They consummated their marriage, and in so doing they conceived a child. Up to that point they had both been virgins. So with just one shot, he produced one life. He was like the opposite of Carlos Hathcock.

T-Bag: I had a roommate on USS *Essex* who proudly went by this call sign. He was a CH-53E pilot who thought it was funny to t-bag his friends when they passed out after drinking one too many. If you don't know what t-bagging someone is, you might want to look up Urban Dictionary on the interwebs. In fact, you might just want to leave that open while you're reading this book. CH-53 pilots are an odd bunch, who look more like auto shop managers than pilots. T-Bag really liked showing off his balls. He'd say, "Check out my new watch!" The victim (sitting down) would naively turn to see the new "watch." Nope! It was not a watch. He also said things like, "Aw, man! I sat in bubblegum." You get the picture. I was the victim on more than one occasion. One time I walked into our stateroom to discover T-Bag completely naked, legs spread from one bed to the next, with his balls hanging down for any unfortunate and unsuspecting soul to see. I have no idea what he was doing, but I can't unsee it. Yeah, his call sign was pretty appropriate.

Shocker: A Harrier pilot was getting out of his jet and somehow caught his wedding ring on the edge of the cockpit as he jumped down to the tarmac. He completely popped his ring finger off from his second knuckle down. So, he got the call sign "Shocker" because, well, Google it. Anyway, Shocker was made to write an article for *Approach*, naval aviation's safety magazine. It's usually a pretty dry read, and it's also very serious. There are no jokes in *Approach* magazine. There is no humor. Shocker's article was published with accompanying photos. In one photo Shocker was standing in front of a Harrier, with an ear-to-ear grin on his face, holding his four-digit hand up next to his chest in its permanent shocker form. Just behind his hand was his leather name tag on his flight suit, which had his newly acquired call sign between his first and middle names printed in gold. How that got past the editor I have no idea.

Batwing: Yeah, there will be more mention of testicles in this book. We're a sophomoric bunch. It's why we became naval aviators—we didn't feel like growing up. I digress. Batwing was an

On USS *Wasp*, they wore masks before it was cool.

F/A-18D back-seater. He was a legend for the way that he could pull and stretch out his ball sack. Why people knew this about him is beyond me. Those who witnessed it said it was freakish. Once you saw it you imagined that when not stretched out it must have hung down to his knees, maybe his ankles. They described his stretched-out ball sack skin as something that looked like a hairy batwing, so naturally a call sign was born. Batwing had a neat bar trick. He could stretch his ball sack out and hold the contents of a pint glass within his batwing without spilling a drop. He used this particular skill to play a little joke on unsuspecting pilots from other squadrons. This required two accomplices. One accomplice would distract the victim, who had just ordered a pint of beer but had yet to drink a drop. While the poor soul was distracted, Batwing would pull his testicles out of his flight suit and would stretch them out as far as he could. The other accomplice would surreptitiously lift the pint of beer from the bar and pour the contents into the stretched-out, hairy, pink skin, all behind the victim's back. Batwing would then pour the beer back into the pint glass and place it back on the bar, before replacing his testicles in his underwear and zipping up his flight suit. Unknowingly the victim would drink the tainted beer, pubes and all. See? Sophomoric.

Face Raper: This one is pretty bad. We don't condone rape of any kind, but somehow the situation called for this call sign. A Marine F-18 squadron was conducting an exercise with US Air Force pilots in South Korea. Having seen the call signs the Air Force pilots had, the Marines decided they needed someone to have a call sign that would shock the delicate sensitivities of their Air Force counterparts. There was a new guy in the squadron. He was a big corn-fed dude. He was told that his call sign for this exercise would be "Face Raper." There was nothing for the young lad to do but salute and turn about smartly. The Air Force pilots were aghast that the Marines would actually give someone the call sign "Face Raper." This was nothing short of psychological warfare. The Air Force pilots were instantly intimidated by these flying leathernecks, who clearly had some marbles loose. Unfortunately for Capt Corn Fed, the name somehow stuck. The problem arose when they tried to paint his call sign on the side of an F-18. That dog was not gonna hunt, so they reduced it to "Face-therapist," but that didn't work either, so it was shortened to "Farap." That worked for a while until Farap got a serious girlfriend and a wedding was planned. She asked him, "Why is your call sign short for face raper?" He didn't have an answer, so a call sign change was approved by the CO. I was not informed as to what his new call sign was.

Ahab: A CH-46E pilot who didn't do well with the ladies in the early hours of the evening would go for the ones he could get. He liked big girls. If you have ever heard of Moby Dick . . . well, you can figure it out.

The Blue Shirts do all the chocking and chaining or unchocking and unchaining of the aircraft that are coming and going. They're all aspiring Yellow Shirts, but you gotta start somewhere.

The dudes in the Green Shirts are the maintainers. When an aircraft breaks or needs scheduled maintenance, the Green Shirts are the guys that provide up-and-ready aircraft for flight operations.

A Marine Corps F-35 mechanic takes a break from the heat in the shade of his jet.

Cosby: Kangaroo courts are known for getting a little out of hand. It's hard to properly describe how much alcohol is consumed, but I believe a rough estimate is a metric shit ton. It's a technical term. Some people get more drunk in less time than others. One reason for this is that it is common practice at K-courts for the beer wenches to spike the beer pitchers with tequila. One major drank too many tequila-laced beers and ended up passing out in the ladies' room. Fast-forward to the next K-court a year later. One of the captains who had been a beer wench at the previous K-court tried to give the major who passed out in the ladies' room a new call sign for having done so. The call sign suggestion he put forth had some traction, but the tables were turned when the major who was the subject of the call sign recommendation blurted out, "Well, if you hadn't been spiking the beer, I wouldn't have passed out!" The CO intervened immediately and announced that the guilty bastard who had spiked the major's drink with tequila would henceforth be named after the most famous of all drink spikers, the one and only Bill Cosby.

P-WE (pronounced Peewee): P-WE was a very attractive MV-22B pilot who was adored by the enlisted personnel in the squadron. Her uniforms were all form fitting, just a touch on the too-tight side of things. Her long blond hair, beautiful smile, and bodacious body culminated in a woman of superior good looks. She was also charming and cheerful. She became a favorite among the enlisted, and it was not uncommon to hear a conversation between two crew chiefs about how hot she was. She was a knockout, and as such she was very Popular with the Enlisted.

HOG: In the sniper world, HOG stands for hunter of gunmen. When a sniper finishes sniper school, they're given a hog's tooth to symbolize their achievement. A Marine Harrier pilot had been a prior enlisted Marine sniper, and he had many stories to tell about hunting Taliban and al-Qaeda in dusty places. His call sign wasn't HOG because he was a hunter of gunmen though. One night while out for a couple of drinks with the squadron at a local Yuma watering hole, HOG approached an attractive lady and began putting on his best moves in an effort to woo her. His efforts were trounced when he suddenly felt the need to vomit and did so all over the pretty lady's high-heeled shoes. HOG stands for Hurls on Girls.

Combat cargo Marines are drawn from the embarked Marine units on board the ship. Each unit has to pay a "tax" in manpower to contribute to embarked operations. Combat cargo Marines are responsible for loading and unloading anything and everything that goes on the ship, no matter what technique is used. The guys in this picture look on as a CH-53E lifts from the deck of USS *Wasp* with an underslung Humvee.

⬟✪⬟ SIMULATED VS. ACTUAL

Inside jokes are the funniest. A somewhat cloistered group of individuals can make a joke that only they will understand, and within that circle the joke is comedic gold. Naval aviation is full of inside jokes; "Pigs in Space" is an example of a naval aviation inside joke. Another is Simulated vs. Actual. Flying isn't always done in an actual aircraft. Each base has very elaborate simulators on hydraulic jacks that simulate the experience of flying in a very realistic way. Pilots and NFOs can simulate training flights in these contraptions and save time and money on real airframes, which are constantly pushed to the limits during actual flights. When you fly in a simulator, the "flight" time is logged into your flight log book as simulated flight time. When you fly in an actual aircraft, the time is logged as actual flight time. Every naval aviator understands this concept. Two Navy MH-60S pilots were carpooling home after a long day at work. One of the pilots lamented to his pal that his wife had been away on business for a very long time, and that he was excited that she was finally coming home the coming weekend. He said, "I am sick of logging simulated time. I am so ready to log some actual!" The simulated vs. actual conundrum was used as a euphemism for the fact that he was getting sick of masturbating (simulated time) and was ready to have sex with his wife (actual time) after a long hiatus.

Combat cargo Marines hook a Humvee underslung load onto the bottom of a hovering CH-53E.

A Navy MH-60S crew chief conducts a preflight of the tail rotor prior to a day of conducting silly circles in the Starboard D.

BOOM: So the story for this guy is that he was pulling duty (it wasn't the only thing he was pulling) as the squadron duty officer (SDO) one lonely Saturday night at MCAS Kaneohe Bay on the island of Oahu. SDO is a twenty-four-hour post. The SDO spends the entirety of the twenty-four hours in the squadron spaces and areas around the base where squadron personnel congregate, such as the barracks, recreational facilities, eateries, etc. The SDO can go get some dinner on base or visit the shoppette for snacks, but otherwise their only form of entertainment is the old magazines kept at the duty desk and Armed Forces Network TV. It's pretty boring duty, especially if performed over a weekend. Nobody calls, nobody visits. The only real excitement is when someone gets in trouble out on liberty and you have to deal with the aftermath and provide a report to the higher headquarters. So the SDO, who happened to be a pretty religious guy, got lonely, got bored, and decided to look up some porn sites on the government computer at the duty desk. Unfortunately for him, a red flag appeared on the computer of the base S-6 officer on the following Monday morning, indicating that someone had looked at an unauthorized website. The name of the perpetrator was easily traced. This is a major no-no; using a government computer to look up porn can ruin a career. Luckily for the horny SDO, he happened to be pals with the S-6 guy. The S-6 guy was happy to make it go away, as long as the horny SDO promised to never do it again. Unfortunately for the SDO, the S-6 guy was also friends with the other officers in the squadron, and word quickly got around that this guy had been wanking off to porn while on duty at a government computer. There were many call sign recommendations, which I will get into momentarily, but the one that was chosen was BOOM, for Beats Off on Mission. Other suggestions included SDO (Stroking Duty Officer), NAPA (Naval Academy Porn Addict), WIFI (Wanks It on Federal Internet), ODO (On-Duty Orgasms), and SINNER (Strokes It Nightly, Never Ever Repents). This last one was especially applicable because BOOM was a very religious guy. That's what you call a plethora of funny call sign recommendations. This story is related to the next story.

FAP: BOOM had a buddy in the squadron who was also a pretty religious guy. When word got out about BOOM's on-duty activities, his buddy approached him in confidence and told him that he too had a problem with porn, and since they went to the same church, maybe they could be partners in their church's accountability program, where people who struggled with porn could keep each other from looking at naughty videos. BOOM agreed. Unfortunately for BOOM's friend, he got caught looking at porn on a government computer shortly after joining forces with BOOM. More unfortunate was the fact that he got caught doing it three times in a ninety-day period. After the third time he was forced out of the squadron and sent to work at the wing headquarters. He didn't leave empty handed though (so to speak), since he was given a call sign to commemorate his time at the squadron. FAP stands for Failed Accountability Program, but it's also the internet's standard sound effect for wanking in written form. Fap Fap Fap Fap Fap Fap . . .

POSTAL: A Marine CH-46E pilot was in Yuma, Arizona, to attend the Weapons and Tactics Instructor Course. When the course was completed and the class was designated as weapons and tactics instructors, they went out to the local strip club to celebrate their momentous achievement. Somehow this married Marine Phrog pilot ended up paying one of his buddy's tabs with his credit card, even though he himself did not partake in the shenanigans that I have been told go on at such establishments. When he got back to his room on the base, he immediately called his wife with an excuse as to why such a charge would appear on their credit card. His call sign was changed to POSTAL: Pays Off Stripper Tab and Lies.

Merlin: No, not Cougar's RIO from *Top Gun*. But I am sure that the inspiration for *Top Gun*'s Merlin was the same as it was for a 1990s-era Navy SH-3 pilot. There was a movie in the early 1980s called *Excalibur*, about the King Arthur legend. King Arthur's wizard was a guy named Merlin, who was

USS *Wasp*, as seen from the ramp of a departing MV-22B, looks like it could use some attention from the needle gunners and a new paint job.

always trying to hook up with a young sorceress who was like, "Stop calling me!" Merlin couldn't get any. Neither could the poor SH-3 guy with the call sign Merlin. Poor Merlin.

Puta: Spanish speakers know this one. It is a derogatory term for a woman who makes her living lying on her back. So a CH-46E pilot somehow earned this unfortunate moniker. I wish I knew the story. Anyway, Puta was told by his squadron mates that his call sign was Spanish for "cool." A Spanish-speaking crew chief knew what puta meant, and assumed that Puta knew what it meant as well, so he asked how Puta got his call sign. "It means 'cool' in Spanish, dude!" The crew chief couldn't stop laughing for the rest of the flight.

Curtains: There was a Navy MH-53 pilot who dyed her hair. Apparently, the dye job was so striking that her fellow aviators were a bit stunned by the change. In typical aviator banter, one of her squadron mates asked if the drapes matched the curtains.

Soapy: Thailand is a beautiful country with beautiful and very friendly women. Some naval aviators over the decades have partaken in some of the more unsavory nighttime attractions in places such as Pattaya, Phuket, and Bangkok while deployed there. One such activity is to take a very soapy bath with a Thai woman, who cleans you with a soapy sponge and does other things. This is called getting a soapy. But Soapy was not one of those naval aviators. In fact, he was a Mormon who was squeaky clean. Never uttered a curse word, never imbibed alcohol, and always remained faithful to his wife. So naturally they gave him his call sign, which everyone associated with prostitution in Thailand, but it was given to a squeaky clean dude. It's ironic, right? Ask Alanis Morissette.

Bukake (pronounced BOO-cake): In Japan, bukake is pronounced boo-KOCK-ee. Don't Google it. It's a thing, and I am not proud that I know what it is (I have an Italian colonel to thank for that). There are people out there who often are the butt of all jokes. They're likable people, but for whatever reason they bring upon themselves chides and jokes and often find themselves being figuratively shot in the face by some well-meaning jokester who does not understand the scars being formed on the inside of the victim. There was a Marine aviator in a squadron stationed in Japan who took so many face shots from his squadron mates that they started calling him Bukake, pronouncing it the Japanese way. The CO did not approve. Not because it might hurt Bukake's feelings, but because you can't say Bukake over the radio in Japan. So the pronunciation was changed to BOO-cake. The CO approved. Poor Bukake, I feel your pain.

MoPed: Back in the 1970s, the Japanese invented a motorized bike that the rider pedaled at first to get it going. They were sort of fun to ride around on, but they weren't something you wanted to have as your sole mode of transportation. In the movie *Hot Rod*, Adam Samberg's character tried to jump a swimming pool on one, for reference. I was told of a Navy P-3 pilot that was not gifted with good looks. Somehow he was okay at convincing women to go to bed with him, but he could never get a girlfriend. In other words, he was fun to ride, but you wouldn't want anyone to see you doing it.

Cletus: I don't mean to disparage southerners, but there is a stereotype that they sometimes marry their cousins; sometimes on purpose and sometimes by accident. There was a Navy P-3 pilot who met a woman at a bar, and they made out like junior high school kids after the dance. They exchanged information and sort of got to staying in touch. When they started sharing details about where they grew up and some of the same people they knew, they discovered a dark family secret. As it so happened, they were second cousins. That ended the burgeoning romance, but it did result in a call sign.

Cinnamon: The night before an MH-60R squadron deployed to the Gulf, the young pilots decided to go out for a night of debauchery at the local strip club. One of these guys took a serious liking to one of the dancers and just kept paying her to give him lap dances. By the end of the night, he was covered in stripper glitter and bronzer. He looked a bit like he'd been sprinkled with cinnamon, and in fact he had. His favorite stripper's stage name was Cinnamon, and from that moment on, so was his.

Buffalo: It's gonna get weird. Have you ever seen *Silence of the Lambs*? There's a scene where Buffalo Bill gets naked and tucks his junk so he can look like a woman as he stares lustily at himself in the mirror. There was an S-3 NFO who got blitzed at a squadron party and decided to do the same thing. Buffalo Bill was too extraneous for talking on the radio. I mean, I've been a pilot in the Marines for a very long time, and this behavior is a little beyond what I would deem as normal. Then again, alcohol is a hell of a drug!

MILF: We all know what that means. There was a Navy EA-18G pilot who was getting married. One of his squadron mates, an NFO, was his best man. The NFO, no doubt in a drunken stupor, had physical relations with the groom's mom at the wedding reception!! MILF told his parents that his call sign stood for "Man! I Love Flying!" It doesn't.

GUE (pronounced gooey): There was a Marine CH-46 pilot who was not particular about the ladies he kept company with. Often his squadron mates would leave the bar empty handed, but not GUE. He had a tried-and-true method for always going home with a woman. He would Go Ugly Early.

CIAO: An F-18 pilot of Italian descent tended to dress a bit provocatively. Her clothing style was based on the principle of less is more. She was known to post pictures on social media that were more revealing than they should have been for a naval officer, so she earned the apropos call sign of CIAO for Clothing Is Always Optional.

WIC: There was a guy in my squadron, a CH-46 pilot, who was always sweating. This was first noticed in the summer of 2007 in Iraq, where the temperature reached ludicrous hot every day. It was even worse when the squadron returned to Okinawa that same summer, where it's not only hot but ludicrously humid. No one knows how he didn't just melt like the Wicked Witch of the West and end up in a puddle on the floor. That guy sweats like a Whore in Church.

Polly: Polly wants a cracker and never shuts up about it. Such was the case of an MV-22 pilot who had the gift of gab. He was like a parrot that spewed meaningless sentences all day long at anyone who passed by. He was also a Mormon. The untrue stereotype about Mormons is that they practice polygamy, which is the real reason Polly was chosen for the Mormon pilot who never shuts up. On a sidenote, I love that the two Mormon pilots in this book fall under the chapter about sex-related call signs.

Tot: An F-18 guy fell head over heels in love with a local gal. They were engaged to be married, until he discovered that she was cheating on him with a guy from another squadron whose call sign was Tater.

SUCK, SQUEEZE, BANG, BLOW

Get your mind out of the gutter! It may sound like someone having a good time on a Saturday night, but it's just a memorization tool to help student naval aviators remember how a jet engine works.

Koncha: In Japan the schoolkids play a fun little game called Koncha. I don't know what Koncha means, so don't ask. Anyway, Japanese kids run around the playground, put their hands together as if holding a pistol, and poke their classmates right up the ass when their classmates aren't looking. Fun game! Right?! Apparently an F-35 pilot in Iwakuni thought so. While drinking at the officers club, he liked to run around and play Koncha with the squadron CO, the MAG CO, the MAW commander, essentially anyone in the room. So he got Koncha for a call sign. When he told me how he had earned his call sign, he said, "How do I tell my parents what my call sign means?" I don't know Koncha, but there's a couple of guys named MILF who may be able to provide a suggestion.

A Marine avionics mechanic conducts checks of the flight instrumentation of an F-35 on a rainy day somewhere on the South China Sea.

CHAPTER 4

CHAPTER 4 WHAT'S IN A NAME?

There's a good *Saturday Night Live* skit starring Nicholas Cage. He and his wife are expecting a baby and trying to select a name. She has a "baby name" book and frustratingly suggests names that her husband shoots down because he can figure out a way to make fun of each name. In her frustration she suggests Beyardker. His eyes light up. He can't think of a way that it could be made fun of. Nothing rhymes with Beyardker, and you can't mispronounce it to get something insulting and degrading. It's perfect! Then the UPS guy knocks on the door. As the husband opens the door, the UPS guy says, "I've got a package for Ass wipe. Is there an Ass wipe here?" The husband, obviously upset, says, "It's Ahz-weep-pay!"

Some people are cursed with terrible names. My last name is Taggart, which is not a terrible last name, but the lovely little douchebags I went to elementary school with liked to call me Faggart. There was a guy on the ship with me whose last name was Dickamore. Luckily for him he was not a pilot or NFO. I once met a Marine major who permanently looked like she could seriously use a vacation. Seriously! Her last name was Dragg . . . as in Major Dragg. If you're unfortunate enough to have a last name that is easy to make fun of, be sure to avoid any career field where the majority of the people never matured past their freshman year in college and who find frat and sorority humor

Recon Marines prepare to board an MV-22B for parachute operations off the coast of Okinawa. They have cool-guy helmets on!

Two recon Marines take a ride in the back of an MH-60 during fast-rope training on board USS *America*.

These guys have the best office view there is.

to be a lot of fun. In case you haven't already figured it out, that includes naval aviation. If you don't care what people call you because of your crappy last name, well, come on in. The water's fine.

Two-bit: Sometimes your call sign is a play on your name. There was a Marine pilot in Okinawa whose last name sounded like whore.

Dumpf: A guy I knew had a squadron commander who'd been around for a while. He was so old, he started as a crew chief in SH-3 Sea Kings, before getting winged and flying as a pilot in one. When my pal knew him, he was a crusty old skipper of an MH-60B squadron. His last name? It was Huck.

Ash: I recently met one of the last remaining Phrog pilots still serving in the Corps from the Give-a-Shit Purple Foxes. It was a bit unprofessional of me to ask him what his call sign story was, given that we were in a meeting to discuss the aviation side of a coming exercise, but his last name lent itself to so many possibilities for a call sign. His last name was Hole. H-O-L-E, Hole. The original call sign suggestion was Glory. Go ahead, Google glory hole; just don't do it at work. However, one of his squadron mates, in a fit of drunken laughter, requested permission to speak during the call sign assignment portion of the Purple Foxes' kangaroo court. Before the body of the court, Hole's squadron mate recommended "Ash," which was received with wide laughter and approval. If you ask me, I would take "Ash" over "Glory" any day of the week. Ash should be thankful for the last-minute save!

Marines fast-rope from the back of the MH-60S on board USS *America*.

Remember when Greyhound earned his call sign for dragging Kuwaiti soldiers into the side of a bus? This is what SPIE rigging looks like.

⊟✪⊟ THE EATERS AND THE EATEN

One cloudy day near Pensacola, the weather went to dog crap. All solo flights were recalled to Saufley Field. As the weather continued to deteriorate, all dual training flights were recalled. The tower made one last call for solos. A solo student naval aviator responded with "Saufley Tower, eat me!" Saufley Tower responded with "Solo flight, consider yourself eaten. You are the only solo flight still flying, and we know who you are." That probably didn't go very well for him when he landed.

Rim: This was given to an MV-22B pilot with an unfortunate last name, especially for someone who joined a profession that uses call signs the way naval aviation does. With the last name of Jobisson, it's just a matter of which you choose for a call sign.

Robert: An F/A-18D pilot had the first name of Robert, and he hated it when people called him Robert. He was constantly correcting people to make them call him Rob. It became a running joke. If a guy reveals his hand like that, he is going to get a call sign that he's going to hate. So his squadron mates gave him a call sign in accordance with the rules of call sign assignment, and that is how he was known henceforth and forever: Rob "Robert" Schmucatelli.

TINCA: An MH-60S pilot came from old money, with links back to the old country. His given name was a family tradition that stretched back centuries but probably didn't sound as bad in the 1600s as it does today. His first name was Dickin. What a terrible name for a pilot to have. Fortunately for

A recon Marine practices shooting drills on the portside aircraft elevator of USS *America*.

Replenishment at sea between USNS *Rappahannock* and USS *Wasp* somewhere on the South China Sea

him, these modern times are not so tolerant of crude call signs. The squadron CO had a hunch that the junior officers would come up with something crude that would surely get him the kind of attention from the wing commander that he would prefer to avoid. All recommendations were shot down, including everyone's favorite, Cider. In frustration the junior officers gave him the call sign TINCA. There Is No Call sign Appropriate.

Dickens: Sort of a twist on the above call sign; there was a Navy F-18 pilot whose last name began with Syder-.

Veiny: I didn't know veiny was an actual word. A CH-53D pilot had the last name of Cox.

Fudge: A Marine CH-46E pilot had the unfortunate last name of Packard.

Pen15: Of course, in the current operating environment you can't just call a dude "Penis." The chief of naval operations would not approve. So a young AH-1W pilot's squadron mates came up with Pen15. If written on the side of an aircraft in all caps it would look like PEN15. How clever. They covered that one up real nice. Not so; it was recognized before a paintbrush stroked the side of an aircraft. He probably ended up with something lame like Gun because his truck had a rifle rack.

S'not/Se7en: There was an F-35 pilot with the last name of Black. Whitest dude you've ever met. So, he's *not* Black. His call sign was eventually changed to Se7en because he had such an odd personality. One strange oddity about him was that he took his Cheerios with orange juice instead of

Two Super Pumas conduct vertical replenishment from USNS *Rappahannock* to USS *Wasp*. These pilots are contracted, but most of them are former US Navy pilots.

milk. He spoke cryptically and often shared "fun facts" about such things as Dante's *Inferno*, medieval torture devices, and odd European customs. Everyone was sure he was a serial killer in real life.

Bo: This seems pretty innocuous at first glance. Even though you think your name is run of the mill and hard to make fun of, sometimes the clever and demented minds of young pilots can find the most unlikely loophole in call sign assignments. Unfortunately for this guy his last name was Kner. Mmm-hmm, you guessed it. Bo-Kner. They probably just called him boner, the pricks!

Pid: Parents don't always think things through. In this case, they should have anticipated the possibility that their son would grow to be a naval aviator. They didn't, though, and they named their son Stuart. He preferred to go by Stu.

Notso: There was a CH-46 pilot with the last name of Smart. Apparently he wasn't particularly bright, so he got the call sign of Notso from the major he worked for. I wonder how he did on his fitness report. There was another guy with the last name of Wise who shared this unfortunate call sign.

Smells: That is a terrible call sign. Oftentimes your last name or first name will inspire an insulting twist of a call sign. In this case, this Marine OV-10 pilot had the unfortunate last name of Gross, and he usually smelled of terrible body odor, so naturally he got the call sign "Smells."

Jeff: It isn't very common, but somehow some pilots make it through years of being a pilot in a sophomoric atmosphere and never pick up a call sign. I know, crazy! Right?! So a guy named Jeff became a squadron commander of an MH-60S squadron and announced to the ready room that it was time for him to get a call sign. That's what you call asking for trouble, but the CO really wanted a call sign. The Junior Officer Protection Agency (JOPA) sprang into action. Many suggestions were offered; many were funny, crude, insulting, offensive, and downright despicable. Scandalous even! A quiet mouse of a pilot was laughing to himself in the corner. The other pilots asked him what he was laughing about. The laughing pilot recommended that his call sign be Jeff. Just Jeff. They reasoned that this would be the one that would bother the CO the most, especially for a guy who had waited his entire career to have his very own call sign. Hey CO, you wanted a call sign, so we will call you Jeff. Junior officers could now call their CO by his first name, and the CO would hate having a call sign that was not really a call sign at all. It stuck. Pure evil genius.

Sick Dick: An East Coast F-14 pilot was named Peter Schmuckatelli III. His fellow JOs, through some alcohol-induced creativity, equated Peter with Dick (Peter being a euphemism for same), and III for ill. It came out as Dick Sick, which had momentum but wasn't quite right. The clever individuals who came up with this call sign racked their brains for a solution. They simply flipped Dick and Sick, and now we have Sick Dick! Sometimes it's necessary to follow the thought process in order to figure out how a call sign was created. I wonder if they got away with putting that on the side of an airplane. Who knows?! It was the '80s, and that decade was crazy!

TAJI GIRL, FUKUOKA GIRL, AND AUSSIE GIRL

Male pilots can be a bit flirtatious sometimes. Put us in the presence of a beautiful woman and we will flirt with her until she says, "Go away, creep!" The same goes for females in air traffic control in certain instances. For instance, in Iraq in 2007 there was a US Army air traffic controller at the Taji air base northwest of Baghdad who had the night shift. If you flew around

During Capt. Colby Howard's time in command of USS *Wasp*, the F-35B underwent its first fully operational tour and conducted many other firsts aboard a ship at sea. USS *Wasp* is the original OG for the F-35B at sea, and Capt. Howard is the original OG.

Anbar Province in 2007, chances are you knew about Taji girl. She had a lovely voice, with a slight huskiness that made her sound like one of those women you can call a 1-800 number and talk dirty to. Now, mind you, we were in Iraq and there wasn't much we could do in regard to sex, so simply talking with a woman who sounded beautiful was enough to make us think she was sexy. She was flirty too. There were definitely some interactions over the comms that skirted the edge of professionalism whenever Marine pilots flew into Taji. We all looked forward to going to Taji simply so we could hear that beautiful voice on the radio. It was a real morale boost.

There was another woman on the radio known as Fukuoka Girl to Navy and Marine pilots who flew the skies of southern Japan. She wasn't flirtatious, and given that we were talking to Fukuoka Center whenever we were speaking with her, we didn't flirt either. But we loved hearing her voice. She had a very high-pitched voice, but when she spoke it was almost as if she was breathing her words as much as saying them. She pronounced her "Ls" with an "R" sound, and the combined effect resulted in a very sexy sound. We all imagined her in her little booth in the basement at Fukuoka Center, surrounded by Pokémon, Hello Kitty, and Disney stuffed animals. Surely she was dressed like the girls in Tokyo with the frilly dresses that are just a little too short and stockings that go to just above the knee. She must have been wearing her hair in pigtails, and between radio calls she sucked on a slightly too-large red lollipop. We hated it when we reached the end of her air space and she passed us off to another controller. We just wanted her to hold us. Hold us as if to put us in holding so we could just listen to her talk on the radio.

Finally, there was a female air boss on HMAS *Canberra* when a buddy of mine was flying around the Pacific back in 2012. None of the US Navy MH-60S pilots who spoke to her on the

radio had any idea what she looked like, but with her sexy Australian accent and her raspy voice, they didn't care. They naturally assumed she was a bombshell from down under. This was especially so because of the lingo the Royal Australian Navy uses for refueling aircraft with engines running. US naval aviators call getting gas with engines running "hot pump." The Royal Australian Navy calls it "hot suck." Imagine being a young US Navy helicopter pilot who's been out at sea for a bit too long and hearing a hot female Australian voice come over the radio saying, "Islander 12, are you inbound for a hot suck?" Whether you needed gas or not, the answer was always "Affirm! Islander 12 is inbound for a hot suck!"

Stool: The F-35B is a state-of-the-art fifth-generation fighter. The pilots selected to fly them are literally the best of the best. The fighter is new, so many of the pilots flying them now are guys who transitioned from Harriers, Hornets, and Prowlers. Their sense of humor still pegs out at middle school. One of their kind had the last name of Sampell. It sounds like "sample," so they made a poo joke out of it and named him "Stool" Sampell.

Big Purple: Some guys grow up dreaming of being naval aviators. It becomes an obsession, a dream that won't die. They stop at nothing until those gold wings are pinned to their chests. Some guys want it so bad that they don't care what their last name is or the myriad of possible call signs that could be derived. When you become a naval aviator and your last name is Weiner, you must have wanted those wings really bad. Big Purple Weiner. As if the last name by itself wasn't bad enough. Poor Weiner.

Squirts: You know, unlike Weiner, an F-14 pilot with the last name of Hershey probably thought his name was pretty safe. He probably thought he'd get a cool call sign like Slick or Razor or some crap Air Force jet pilots give each other. But someone somewhere came up with a euphemism for diarrhea: Hershey Squirts. So, yeah . . .

Israel: I don't have anything against the LGBT community. I've watched a lot of *Will and Grace*, I am perfectly good with Dumbledore being a gay man, and I am a big fan of people living their lives the way they want to as long as it's not hurting anyone. The point is, I was once homophobic because of the way I was raised (you get programmed) and WHEN I was raised, but I am very much over it. So I apologize up front if this story offends any of my LGBT brothers and sisters, but please try to view it as lighthearted, immature, and sophomoric (like most of naval aviation), and not anti-LGBT. Here goes! There was a Navy MH-60S pilot whose last name was Egay. Someone really put some effort into his call sign and assigned him with Israel. You don't get it, I understand. I didn't get it either. However, when his name was written out on the side of his aircraft as Mike "Israel" Egay, if read correctly, it sounded like Mike is really gay. He wasn't gay, "not that there's anything wrong with that."

Tits: I was hoping this one was going to be an acronym, but I wasn't necessarily disappointed in the actual reason for this call sign. Before I go any further, it should be noted that when I asked a young MV-22 pilot what his call sign was and why he had it, I did not know his name. He was wearing his leather flight jacket over his flight suit, and his leather name patch was not seen. His last name was McGee. Tits was a no-brainer. Tits McGee was made famous in *Anchorman*, when Ron Burgundy used it to make fun of his coanchor. According to street lingo, it's slang for a woman who has large breasts. Tits McGee is not very clever, but it is simple and refined, like naval aviation.

USS *Wasp*, USS *America*, and other ships in the amphib Navy exist to support Marine grunts. All the flight operations on board USS *Wasp* and *America* ultimately supported grunts like the ones pictured here.

Parade rest! A sailor mans the rails during a port visit to Singapore.

It's all rainbows and unicorns on board USS *Wasp*.

Dick: This is at least in the top five worst call signs I have ever heard. In the military there's a euphemism for the hand a man uses to masturbate with. That hand is called a dick skinner. If you've ever watched the movie *Platoon*, there's a scene where Chris (Charlie Sheen) is ordered to dig a foxhole. A soldier called "Junior" barks at Chris, "Hey, man! That hole ain't gonna dig itself. Getchya dick skinner on that thing. Dig! Dig!" Dick was a Cobra pilot, and you can probably guess what his last name was.

Hairball: This call sign story has a surprise ending! A Navy CH-46D pilot earned the call sign "Hairball" during his first fleet tour. After completing an out-of-cockpit tour and returning to his old squadron as a department head, he noticed that call sign suggestions were showing up on his page in the Charge Book. He stupidly informed the JOs in his squadron that he had already received the call sign "Hairball" and there was no need to go through the trouble of finding him a new one. This was a huge mistake. Fighting to keep the call sign you have is not the hill you want to die on. The major misstep this guy took was letting it be known that he was happy with "Hairball." The squadron JOs changed Hairball's call sign to something he definitely did not like. He is now forever known as "Ball Hair."

⊕ WORDS HAVE MEANING

Some student naval aviators struggle through flight school. I know a guy! One student naval aviator was having a rough flight. He just couldn't do anything right with his T-34 Turbo Mentor training aircraft. He was forgetting his emergency procedures, couldn't perform a high- or low-altitude precautionary landing, and his practice landings weren't great. While executing some practice EPs, he fell so far behind the aircraft that he blurted out, "I'm a f**king moron" on the ICS . . . or so he thought. Actually he transmitted his frustration on Center's frequency because he forgot to make sure his comm switch was in the ICS detent. Center immediately responded with "Last aircraft that transmitted, say call sign." Before the student could incriminate himself, the instructor came on the radio and said, "He said he was a f**king moron, not that he was f**king stupid!" Center did not press the issue.

This could be a recruiting poster for the Navy / Marine Corps team. It's not, but it could be . . . (hint, hint)

A shitter comes in for a landing behind a spinning playmate on board USS *Wasp*.

Two Marines provide aerial sniper coverage from the back of an airborne MH-60S during a visit board search-and-seizure exercise on the South China Sea.

VMF 121

CHAPTER 5

CHAPTER 5 | THIS IS THE CRAPPIEST CHAPTER YOU WILL EVER READ

I am convinced that jet pilots are more prone to crapping themselves than other pilots. You'll read two epic stories below about a couple of guys named Birdbath and PIMP. Both were Harrier pilots and both guys soiled themselves: one in the cockpit, and one in the head. Here's the thing: jet guys often fly for hours on end. Over Afghanistan and Iraq they fly silly circles in the sky while waiting for a joint terminal attack controller on the ground to call some steel rain in, yo-yoing back and forth to the tanker for gas, and oftentimes returning to the base or their carrier after hours of circling overhead without dropping a single bomb. Well, some have dropped bombs of another sort, but I'll get to that in a bit.

I doubt there are too many P-3 or C-130 pilots out there who have crapped themselves while flying, because both of those aircraft are equipped with toilets. Hell, they got fridges, and microwaves, and midgets to serve cappuccinos and snacks. They're spoiled bastards. The only thing jet guys have to relieve themselves is a rubber relief tube that has a funnel on the end to catch all of their urine when they drain the main vein, if they're lucky; female jet pilots and NFOs have it even worse. Some jets don't even have that, and the pilots and NFOs have to bring "piddle packs" in case they need to relieve themselves. What pilots and NFOs in tiny little cockpits don't have is a way to vacate their bowels unless they come up with a clever and ingenious way to do so. Most do not. There was a Marine single-seat

MV-22Bs parked in the forward "Slash"

An LSE directs a Marine UH-1Y Huey in for a landing. The UH-1Y is the latest installment of the Huey, a legacy that stretches all the way back to before the US entrance into the Vietnam War.

The SAR bird pops in for a splash of gas and a crew swap.

Hornet pilot who managed to poo into a ziplock baggie once. He "safed" the ejection seat, unstrapped, undid his G-suit, shimmied out of his flight suit, then somehow contorted himself so he could do the deed. How he did this while still flying the jet is anyone's guess. It wasn't as if the F-18 NATOPS had a note, warning, or caution stating that "pilots and NFOs shall not take a dump while flying." He's a very exceptional exception. Helicopter pilots are not completely immune to getting their bodily excretions all over themselves, but for the most part a rotor wing pilot can land the helicopter and do a "stub wing check" or wander off behind a tree to "soft duck" some "SEALs."

There is a naval aviation axiom that I just made up that goes something like this. There are three types of naval aviators/naval flight officers: (1) those who have crapped themselves before, during, or after a flight, and everyone knows about it, (2) those who have crapped themselves in one of the previously mentioned flight regimes, but no one knows about it, and (3) those who WILL crap themselves before, during, or after a flight. Although this chapter is dedicated to pilots and NFOs who have crapped themselves, it is also the catchall for other bodily fluids that have been released at inopportune times. This chapter also covers urine, puke, and even periods. It's a celebration of the disgusting functions of the human body and the pilots and NFOs who have had unfortunate encounters with their own biological processes. This is their story. This chapter is dedicated to all naval aviators and naval flight officers who have paid the ultimate price while in the performance of their dooties.

Birdbath: There were two AV-8B Harrier pilots whose mission was to fly their jets from USS *Peleliu*, stationed off the coast to a military range in Southern California, drop some bombs, and then return to "mother" (the ship). As the section leader climbed into his cockpit, he felt a little grumbling in his stomach. Reasoning that the flight would be only forty-five minutes long, he elected to wait to make a head call and strapped into his jet. After all, getting in and out of a G-suit isn't exactly easy. Unfortunately for him, his launch was delayed due to a broken helicopter on the tramline, and they launched forty-five minutes later than planned. Eventually, the Harrier section was given a green deck for launch, and off the two pilots flew into the wild blue yonder. As the section of Harriers crossed the beach into California, the dash-two pilot noticed that his section leader's plane seemed to sort of wobble through the sky. Dash Two called his section leader and asked if everything was

okay. The section leader responded somewhat gruffly that he was fine and that they should continue the mission. Over the bombing range they went, dropping their bombs, before flipping a U-turn to return to the ship. As they crossed the beach on the way back to mother, the section leader's plane began to wobble again, this time more so. Dash-two asked what the issue was, and the section leader's response must have come as a bit of a surprise. "Dude, I've crapped myself!" Not just once, but twice, and it was a smelly disaster in his cockpit. The section leader made the decision to divert to Naval Air Station North Island on Coronado Island in San Diego, because he could not bring himself to return to mother in his current condition. The section of Harriers peeled north and approached North Island. After an uneventful landing, the section leader taxied in at 70 mph. Per OPNAVINST 3710, aircraft are not supposed to taxi any faster than an average person can jog. Dash-two arrived on the visiting aircraft line to discover that his wingman had already shut his Harrier down, exited the aircraft, and run into base ops. Once he had shut down his own Harrier, dash-two climbed the ladder to his section leader's aircraft and discovered, most unpleasantly, the poo disaster that was his section leader's cockpit. Dash-two followed the trail into base ops and into the head. He discovered a poo-covered gear explosion. There was poo everywhere; a crap-covered flight glove here, a poo-covered kneeboard there, a soiled G-suit near the stalls, and other accoutrements of flying gear all over the place, all covered in human feces. Continuing to follow the trail, dash-two discovered his section leader in the handicap stall completely naked except for one boot and his flight suit strung out behind him, covered in excrement. The section leader was straddling the toilet, facing the wall, and splashing toilet water up onto his undercarriage like a bird in a birdbath, in a desperate attempt to remove the splattered poo from his naked body. The two pilots worked together for two hours to clean up the mess in the bathroom and in the cockpit. Once done, they checked themselves into the

Just another pretty sunset at sea. Sometimes you look out at a sunset on the open ocean, and you believe for a split second that the whole ocean is on fire.

Ooh, look at the pretty clouds!

Navy Lodge for the night, since it had become too late to return to mother. Sitting down at dinner in the Gas Lamp district of San Diego, the section leader asked his wingman to keep what had happened between them. Lead was concerned about his reputation, and he liked the call sign he already had. He was sure a call sign change would occur if this story leaked. Dash-two gave his word not to tell a soul. The next day they departed North Island and returned to mother. Five minutes after shutting down and climbing out of his aircraft, Lead was in the flight equipment room turning in his gear. The sergeant behind the counter saw the section leader and blurted out, "Hey sir, I heard you shit yourself!" So much for secrets between friends! Since the section leader thought it was a good idea to use a toilet bowl as a birdbath, his call sign was forever changed to "Birdbath," and old Birdbath entered the pages of call sign legend.

Flight ops on USS *Wasp*. The MV-22B in the foreground is seen here in the middle of a crew swap.

⬟★⬟ TOILET PAPER BOMBS

Back in the old days, "when men were men and goats were afraid," they flew a beast of an aircraft called the T-28 at flight school. The T-28 was a massive single-engine propeller-driven airplane, which I am told was a bear to fly. It had air brakes that could be extended by the pilots to slow the aircraft down, since it weighed so much and the wheel brakes needed all the help they could get when landing. The air brakes were essentially flat surfaces that could be extended out from both sides of the fuselage to create drag and slow the aircraft. These air brakes were also used for some prelanding shenanigans. When the air brakes were stowed, there was enough space underneath the surfaces to stash flattened rolls of toilet paper. Upon returning from a training flight, the pilot would open the air brakes and bomb the field duty officer shack with harmless rolls of toilet paper. This was common and all fun and games until it almost got someone hurt. An instructor pilot loaded his air breaks with toilet paper bombs and took his student up for anThe last part of this story is missing. "...instrument flight. At altitude they flew through clouds and the toilet paper rolls got wet. They also froze into solid chunks of rolled death as the freezing layer was much lower than usual. As the T-28 came in for its "bombing run" the air brakes were opened, and solid chunks of toilet paper ice rolls went smashing into the FDO shack. The FDO ran for his life and the shack was completely destroyed. That was the end of toilet paper bombing at flight school. Nice bombing run, though. "

instrument flight. At altitude they flew through clouds, and the toilet paper rolls got wet. They also froze into solid chunks of rolled death, since it was February and the freezing layer was much lower than usual. As the T-28 came in for its "bombing run," the air brakes were opened and solid chunks of toilet paper ice rolls went smashing into the FDO shack. The FDO ran for his life and the shack was completely destroyed. That was the end of toilet paper bombing at flight school. Nice bombing run, though.

This CH-53E is getting some bounces in during "pinkie" time.

UNIC (Eunic): After a long night of drinking while on liberty in Pusan, Korea, an E-2C Hawkeye pilot felt the urge to drain the main vein. He somehow managed to stumble to the bathroom of the back-alley bar he and his squadron mates were drinking in, so he could tinkle. One of his squadron mates also had to pee, and upon entering the men's room he found the drunk E-2C pilot peeing in the corner next to a urinal. In the morning, the now-hung-over E-2C pilot had no recollection of needlessly peeing in a corner directly adjacent to a perfectly good urinal. UNIC stands for Urinates Needlessly in the Corner.

POOTS: One night in Bangkok can make a hard man humble. Especially when you mix Thai food and alcohol. A C-12 pilot returned to his hotel room after a night on the town in Bangkok, and he needed to take a BM in the worst way. He sat on the toilet to do just that and subsequently passed out right there on the seat, middump. He was found there the next day by his buddy, who was let in by the maid. The maid was unfazed, by the way. I mean, it's Bangkok. POOTS stands for Passed Out on Toilet Seat.

SHILOC: A Navy Hornet pilot took off from the ship with a strike package on its way to Fallujah from an aircraft carrier stationed in the Persian Gulf. A strike package can be any combination of aircraft launched from a ship to strike enemy targets; in this case it was F-18s, EA-6Bs, E-2 Hawkeyes, etc. Now, when aircraft launch from a ship on a combat mission, there is a ready deck, or standby aircraft that are manned and started, ready to launch if an aircraft in the strike package is unable to do so or has to immediately return to the ship in an emergency. Once all aircraft are airborne and good to go, the ready deck stands down and the pilots shut down their aircraft and head into the ready room. About thirty minutes after this strike package had departed for Iraq, one of the package F-18 pilots called the tower, requesting a ready deck. He declared an emergency and requested immediate handling for landing. The tower asked the pilot what the nature of his emergency was, and was told that the emergency was physiological. At the time, there had been a rash of in-flight problems with the aircraft oxygen systems, so immediately the air boss was concerned that the pilot might not be getting enough oxygen and, depending on his altitude, might become hypoxic. Hypoxia is when the brain doesn't get enough oxygen, which could result in a pilot blacking out at the controls of a multimillion-dollar aircraft. Not good. The air boss started asking questions such as "What's your altitude?," "What is your heading?," etc. Each time the pilot responded crisply and concisely, indicating that he was alert and likely did not have a problem with his oxygen system. "What is the nature of your emergency?" asked the air boss. The pilot responded, "Physiological," but provided no further details. Once the pilot was cleared to enter the break, he decided to enter the downwind immediately, forgoing the standard break turn over the front of the ship, which raised an eyebrow or two in the tower. By this time, the entire ship was aware that there was an incoming aircraft with an emergency, and everyone had been called to general quarters. The crash crew had rolled out in full force to respond to whatever the emergency was. Suddenly the pilot, still on the downwind leg of his landing, told tower, "Never mind; cancel the emergency," with a touch of frustration in his voice. The pilot trapped with no issue and taxied into his parking spot. A school circle of deck crew had gathered around the cockpit, waiting for the pilot to open the canopy and climb out. The crash crew and medical personnel were there in full force to respond to whatever the physiological emergency was. Everyone on the flight deck and in the tower was watching, waiting to see what caused the pilot to announce an emergency. The canopy remained closed, even after the pilot had shut down the engine and the crew ladder had been lowered. Meanwhile in the cockpit, the pilot was flailing his arms about. He had removed his helmet and he was wriggling and writhing in his cockpit, but no one could figure out what his problem was or what he was doing. After seven long minutes, the pilot put his helmet back on his head and opened the canopy. To everyone's shock, he stood up in the cockpit and climbed

out onto the crew ladder wearing nothing but his boxer shorts, T-shirt, helmet, and flight boots. To this day, people wonder how he got his flight suit off while wearing his flight boots. Under his arm was a bundle of flight gear, including his G-suit, flight suit, parachute harness, survival vest, etc. Once on the deck he walked briskly over to the side of the ship and heaved all of it into the ocean with a flare of great disgust and frustration. He then walked off the flight deck with as much dignity as he could muster, without a word to anyone. The maintenance personnel said the inside of the cockpit looked like a monkey cage that had been neglected for too long. SHILOC stands for Shit Himself in Lieu of Combat. It's too bad—he almost made it back to the ship before he lost control of his bowels. So close!

SOFIH (pronounced Sophie): Patton once said that "a good plan, violently executed now, is better than a perfect plan next week." Well, a young MV-22 pilot had neither a good plan nor a perfect one, but violent execution was in his very immediate future. After stumbling back to his Honolulu hotel room after having way too much to drink, he was viciously attacked by the Double Dragon, and he had little time to decide which end was the priority. He chose poorly. Sitting on the toilet, he realized that he was going to puke first. Most people, I think, would have stayed on the toilet and thrown up in the tub. Not this guy. He sprang from the toilet, his pants around his ankles, and immediately vomited into the bowl. As he did so, the other side of the dragon pounced. He shat all over himself and the bathroom floor. The attack of the Double Dragon lasted a couple of minutes before the beast took pity and left him in a poo-covered heap on the white-tiled floor. At some point in the night, he made a feeble attempt at cleaning himself up, wiping himself and the bathroom floor with a single hand towel, which he then shoved under the sink. He was discovered the next day by his squadron mate, head in the toilet, still covered by his own excrement. Alcohol is fun, kids! SOFIH stands for Shat on Floor in Hotel.

All the colors of the rainbow on display during nighttime F-35B carrier qualification

Hat Trick: According to the Google dictionary, a hat trick is three consecutive successes within a limited span of time. If a soccer or hockey player scores three goals in a game, it's called a hat trick. I am not entirely sure that this story qualifies under the above definition, since there is nothing successful about what you are about to read. An E-2C NFO went into Bahrain for liberty and was viciously attacked by the Double Dragon. In the space of one evening, he managed to soil himself not once, not twice, but three times! Alcohol may have played a decisive role in this misadventure. He was three sheets to the wind by the time he crapped himself the first time. The hat trick was the worst. He was found that night curled up in the fetal position on the floor of the men's head in a puddle of his own excrement and vomit. I don't think you can call that three consecutive successes; three somethings, but not successes.

SITS: Look, I warned you that this was a disgusting chapter. So is this call sign. A Navy MH-60R pilot got so drunk one night while in port that he didn't really know what was what. Stumbling back to his stateroom, he decided he needed a shower. Forgetting to slip on his shower shoes (believe me, you don't want to take a shower barefoot on a ship), he stripped down, grabbed his towel, and wandered off to the head. In the shower, all soaped up and lathered, he vacated his bowels on the shower floor without quite realizing what he had done. When he noticed a turd on the shower floor that hadn't been there when he got into the shower, he surmised that it must be his. Sometimes we do strange things in a panic. Worried that he might be caught and forever known as the guy who shat in a shower, he did the only thing he could do. Apparently, his solution actually has a name because it happens often enough. "Waffle stomping" is when you attempt to squash the poo down the drain with your feet, in this case bare feet. You may have seen some drains in a locker room shower that are circular in shape with drain holes shaped like tiny squares in neat rows, like a waffle. Unfortunately the stomper was caught midstomp, since he had forgotten to close his shower curtain, and one of his squadron mates saw what he was doing. SITS stands for Shits in the Shower. He will literally be forever known as "the guy who shat in the shower."

Squats: On the ship I was assigned while writing the majority of this book, I worked with a Marine Expeditionary Unit air officer with the call sign Scallywag. He was a really good storyteller and had lots of good stories to tell about flying in the ugliest jet known to man, the EA-6B Prowler. Many of the Prowler stories in this book were provided by him. One such story was that of Squats. A Prowler pilot earned this call sign one day on the tarmac at Bagram Air Base in Afghanistan, when he urgently needed to drain the main vein but didn't know where he could go other than near his aircraft. Not wanting to be spotted whizzing all over the US Air Force's pristine tarmac, he sort of squatted down by one of the main landing-gear tires, worked his penis out of his flight suit, and let loose a stream of urine. Aircraft aren't supposed to leave puddles like the one this guy left, and when one of the Air Force ground crew noticed the pool of mystery fluid that had formed under the Marine EA-6B, he assembled a cleanup crew and showed up at the jet to clean up the mess. Needless to say, the embarrassed pilot was busted, and he earned his call sign the old-fashioned way.

Gator: I don't know the story behind Gator's call sign. I flew UC-12 King Airs with him while we were both assigned to the station squadron at Marine Corps Air Station Futenma in Okinawa, Japan. He reminded me of Lt. Col. Wilbur "Bull" Meechum, played by Robert Duvall in *The Great Santini*. *The Great Santini* was a movie based on a real Marine F-4 pilot who was God's gift to Marine fighter jocks. Robert Duvall's portrayal of the "Great Santini" was a spot-on image of a cocky Marine jet pilot. Bull was adored by women, chagrined by the brass, and loved by his men. He was always cracking jokes and was never one to shy away from pranks and hijinks. That was Gator. Gator even looked like Robert Duvall, with a shit-eating grin and a receding hairline cut into a tight Marine medium regulation style. He was a rare breed among naval aviators. His career started in the back

A long exposure shows the F-35B hovering in for a landing on USS *Wasp.*

of Prowlers as an NFO, but he always wanted to be a pilot. He put in for a pilot transfer and ended up getting jet scores. He of course selected the Prowler. The Prowler is pointy in the back and bulbous at the nose, with a large, extended air-refueling probe that juts out just in front of the cockpit. It is the loudest jet in the world! Some people sort of resemble the aircraft they fly, and the same can be said of ol' Gator. As it turns out, he was a pretty damn good pilot. He had a swagger about him that seemed to keep him out of a lot of trouble even if he was always stirring trouble up. Scally said he was nasty in the cockpit. He chewed tobacco and got it all over the knobs and instruments. When he was done relieving himself in the piss tube, he would shake the tube out on the multifunction display and laugh like a kid pulling some trick on his buddy. One time he used the piss tube while taxiing in from a flight, and the guys in the jet behind him thought Gator's jet was leaking fuel. "Hey, Gator, I think you've sprung a leak!" Gator just came over the radio with his signature, hushed laugh. The other guys would laugh and shake their heads.

Shaggy and **SCOOBE** (Scooby): Shaggy is so named because he looks like Shaggy from the cartoon *Scooby Doo*. SCOOBE is so named because he had irritable bowel syndrome. He also had the annoying habit of talking about IBS all the time. We get it, dude; you have IBS. One day Shaggy and the man who would become SCOOBE were on a training flight in an MH-60S Seahawk helicopter. The IBS monster reared its ugly head and Shaggy's copilot disastrously shat in his flight suit and then threw up all over himself. So, Shaggy's copilot had Shit Coming out of Both Ends.

Starfish: During a kangaroo court, one of the beer wenches had taken his beer wench uniform a little further than his fellow beer wenches. The uniform was a grass skirt and coconut bra or shirt tied up the way women sometimes do. Most of the beer wenches wore shorts under their grass skirts. Not this guy. He wore a jockstrap, and on his ass he wrote the squadron's moniker for all to see. He spent the night going around to tables and taking drink orders while talking out his ass à la Ace Ventura, showing his brown starfish off to his customers. Brown starfish was extraneous on the radio, so . . .

Poodini: It rhymes with Houdini, get it? Jet guys and poo, they go together like peas and carrots. As I have already pointed out, the EA-6B Prowler may very well be the ugliest jet airplane ever created. The pointy end is facing the wrong way, for one, and the nose of the aircraft looks like a ball sack. The Prowler has four seats, two up front and two in the back. The pilot is outnumbered by NFOs three to one. Sometimes, though, Prowlers will fly with a pilot and NFO up front and one NFO in back. There was an NFO who had a gift for going poo in the back seat without anyone noticing. You have to understand that going number two in the back of a jet is an arduous task, especially in the back seat of a Prowler, which was made for midgets. First of all, you have to "safe" the ejection seat; accidentally ejecting with your butt hanging out of your flight suit while you empty your bowels will get you more than a call sign. You also have to unstrap from the seat, undo your G-suit, shimmy out of your flight suit, and then contort yourself like Houdini in some way that allows you to take care of business, all in a very compact space. To do this without the guys up front noticing takes sheer will and a lot of skill. Poodini somehow managed this feat at least twice. The only reason anyone knows is because he liked to throw the ziplock baggies he shat in up into the forward part of the cockpit when he was done.

Wizz: When you first join the military, and I think this especially applies to the Marines, you get treated terribly by your superiors. Whether it's drill instructors at boot camp, sergeant instructors at officer candidate school, or instructor pilots at flight school, you just get sort of used to being verbally berated by superior officers. You're new, you suck, and therefore you deserve to be treated like a misbehaved

child. When a young F/A-18D (two-seat version of the F/A-18) nonflying officer showed up to his squadron, he was expecting to be treated like he'd always been treated. On his first flight as a WSO (weapons systems officer) in his squadron, he was immediately intimidated by his pilot, who was a grizzled old major. Being new, the young WSO forgot to bring a "piddle pack." He discovered, to his great discomfort, that he really had to go pee. Unfortunately for him, there were still two hours to go before landing, and he was too afraid to ask the pilot if he could borrow a "piddle pack." Long story short, he had no choice but to relieve himself in his flight suit. Once the flight was over, everyone from the flight line to flight equipment noticed that the WSO had wet himself, and he was instantly infamous for his lack of bladder control. His call sign is Wizz for the above-described embarrassing incident, but it's a play on the fact that he is also a WSO, which is pronounced Wiz-oh.

Puddles: There was a Marine F-18 NFO flying a very long flight over Iraq on a dark and moonless night. It was so dark that the pilot and NFO could barely see their hands in front of their faces, let alone what they were doing with their hands. The NFO had to go pee, so he opened his helmet bag, pulled out a "piddle pack," and let loose a long stream of hot urine. His aim was a bit off. Instead of filling the "piddle pack," he pissed all over his flight suit leg and filled the many recesses of the cockpit floor with puddles of urine; thus the call sign.

🇺🇸 THE TROUBLE WITH THE "HEADS" ON THE BOAT

On the ship there are various departments and divisions that all "own" spaces for which the personnel within those departments and divisions are responsible for maintaining and cleaning. This includes male and female heads. Oftentimes these bathroom facilities are located in high-trafficked areas, and sailors and Marines who don't work in those areas will use these heads without any consideration for the sailors and Marines who have to clean them. So the salty chiefs and gunnies lock these heads to prevent "nonessential" personnel from making a nasty mess in their heads. In some cases, they will have the toilet seats removed from the male heads so that you can only urinate in the toilet. This prevents the necessity to clean someone else's poo streaks from the bowl. I have told you about the high security placed on heads in high-trafficked areas so that you will understand the predicament the pilot in our next call sign story found himself in on a dark and stormy night out at sea . . .

PIMP: A Harrier pilot on a ship was getting ready to take off into the murky black ink of night for some nighttime CQs (carrier qualification landings). It was the last day of the month, and he had to complete the CQs or he was going to lose currency, which would require a lot more landings with proper lunar illumination and so on. Essentially, if he didn't get his night landings, he was going to cause a major headache for the squadron operations officer and himself. Unfortunately for this Harrier pilot, he suffered from Crohn's disease, which sometimes causes a person to go number two at the most-inopportune times. As he left the ready room to walk to his jet, he felt the all-too-familiar rumbling in his stomach. He called his operations officer and begged him to delay his takeoff so he could vacate his bowels. The answer was no. It was a now-or-never situation, since the flight deck would be closed in an hour and a half. Either he launched on time or he didn't launch at all, due to the fast-approaching end to the flight window. So the pilot climbed into his jet and strapped in. He started the engines and waited for his turn to launch. Suddenly he felt a rumbling again, but it was much stronger this time. He knew he would have to drop the kids off in the very near future. He called the squadron representative in the tower and asked to delay his flight so he could visit the loo.

Elton strikes a pose in his "Green Knights" sport coat on a yacht somewhere in the Gulf of Thailand.

The "Green Knights" enjoying a little leisure time in Thailand

The answer was "Negative, ghost rider." This was his only chance to knock out these landings. So he resigned himself to a very uncomfortable forty-five-minute flight. As the LSE (landing signal, enlisted) signaled for the pilot to taxi forward for launch, the pilot felt the battle raging in his stomach, and knew he could not wait. He waived off the LSE, shut the jet down, leapt from his cockpit, and rushed to find a head. The first head he came to was locked. Apparently the head had just been cleaned, and the chiefs on the boat didn't want it to be blemished before it was inspected. Rushing on to the next head, the pilot discovered to his dismay that it too was locked. He ran like a sprinter to the officer's head near his room. Unbuckling and unstrapping his flight gear as he went, the pilot knew the situation was desperate, and he didn't think he was going to make it. Finally reaching the bathroom, he struggled to drop his flight suit, but it was too late. He crapped all over himself and made an absolute mess of his flight suit. Sitting in the bathroom stall, trying to clean himself up, the pilot suddenly saw flashes coming from above him. Looking up, he saw his squadron mates looking down at him with cameras, snapping shots of the young pilot's lost dignity. Later, after cleaning himself up and changing into a fresh flight suit, the Harrier pilot went to the ready room for an all-officers meeting. He was the last to enter. As he came into the ready room, his fellow pilots began a slow clap building into a crescendo. A new call sign was bestowed. He would forever be known as PIMP for Pooped in My Pants. I know it's childish, but so are pilots.

POMPOM: It was a dark and stormy night off the coast of Norfolk, Virginia. A single MH-60S went out for a night search-and-rescue training mission. The helicopter aircraft commander was a very serious dude. Because the water was cold, the crew had to wear their poopy suits, or wet/cold-weather suits, in case they crashed in the frigid water and had to wait a little while for their rescue. In the case of the HAC, the poopy suit would become appropriately named. The HAC soiled himself, and it was all trapped in his poopy suit. Not wanting to incur a mission failure, the HAC sucked it up, told no

one else in the helicopter of his unfortunate situation, and pressed on mission. At mission completion, the helicopter landed safely at home base, and the crew got ready for the debrief. The HAC was late to the debrief, which was unusual for him. Eventually, he arrived and provided a professional debrief of the mission, announcing at one point that he had had a little accident in his pants during the flight ("Come again?"). The other crew members asked why he didn't just land somewhere and relieve himself or get himself cleaned up. It was, after all, only a training mission. The HAC stated that he didn't want to interrupt the mission and chose to press. So someone came up with POMPOM, Pooped on Myself Pressed On Mission.

Mush Pants: If you've ever seen *South Park*, you may be familiar with the character "Mush Pants Mehlman," so called because he pooped himself all the time. Mush, as I knew him, was the mini boss on USS *Wasp*, and his last name happened to be Mehlman. Good dude, solid officer. He was definitely going places. However, we on the ship were all under the impression that his call sign was simply Mush because of some reason other than what he got it for. To me, in my desire to collect call sign stories, the story he offered was not funny enough to be included in the book and certainly not very memorable, because I have completely forgotten it. Then I ran into one of his old squadron buddies, who told me how Mush really got his call sign (see note below). At his squadron's kangaroo court, his squadron mates wanted to capitalize on Mehlman's name, which he shared with the character on *South Park*. So, they circulated a story that he had shat his flight suit while flying, and the story sort of spread throughout the entire wing. However, old Mush never shat himself, at least not that anyone knows about. He earned his call sign simply because of his name and a nasty rumor. He hated that call sign, and per the rules of call sign assignment, the hated call sign naturally stuck. Love ya, Mush! (*Note*: I got this story from Video, whom you've already read about. When I told Mush that Video had revealed

An F-35B takes off into the sunset on board USS *Wasp*.

the true meaning of his call sign, Mush got his revenge and told me what Video's call sign was really about. For the record, I had been told that Video's call sign was Grimace. Apparently, Video didn't like his call sign very much, so he was telling people that his call sign was Grimace.

THE PISS TUBE

The CH-46E is equipped with piss tubes for the pilot and copilot. Phrog pilots didn't usually use them, because they could just land and check the stub wing for leaks. However, during long flights overwater, there was nowhere to land, and if you gotta go, you gotta go. An OpsO in a 46 squadron discovered much to his severe chagrin the truth about helicopter piss tubes. When the avionics mechanics climb into the cockpit to fix whatever equipment in the cockpit is broken (it's always something), they're up there for a long time. Many of these yokels chew tobacco, and with nowhere else to spit they sometimes use the piss tube. Over time the piss tube gets clogged with tobacco sputum, which brings us back to our story. The OpsO was in the right seat, which in the Phrog is where the HAC sits. He had to piss and he had to piss immediately. So he reached under his seat, grabbed the piss tube, squeezed the trigger (this is what creates the suction that dumps the urine overboard), and let loose a long stream of pee. The problem arose when there was no suction and the funnel cup at the top of the piss tube filled with urine. The OpsO had to pinch it off because the urine was to the brim. He didn't know what to do in this particular aircraft emergency. Piss tube malfunction is not covered in NATOPS. His only solution, it seemed, was to throw it out the window. He used his free hand to open the side window and attempted to chuck his pee out into the airstream. The piss tube hose goes only so far. It was far enough for him to get the urine to the window, but not far enough to get the urine out of the window. In fact, there's a weird aerodynamic glitch to the side window in the cockpit. Somewhere close to the window or just short of it, there is a slipstream that actually blows air back into your face. So instead of dumping his piss out the window, he sprayed it all over himself and the copilot. They still had another two hours of flight time before they landed at their next fuel stop.

Big Bird: On a Saturday in Atsugi, Japan, there was a young Navy MH-60 pilot who went big and drank more than he could handle. Let's back up. There is a fast-food joint all over Japan known as Coco's Curry. It is Japanese curry and it tastes amazing. Imagine half of a plate covered in Japanese rice, the other half filled with Japanese curry, with deep-fried meat of some sort in the middle, with delicious flat bread for dipping in the curry, and topped off with melted cheese. People who have lived in Japan know. Anyway, this MH-60 pilot was on a bender. He was drinking Japanese beer and Chew-Hi's like they were gonna run out or something, and after eating a large plate of Coco's famous curry, he and his buddies headed to the Atsugi officers club to continue what can only be described as stupidly excessive drinking. After more beers than anyone could count, our pal ordered a large beer at the bar and drank it down in one go. He slammed the beer mug on the bar and immediately regretted this decision. To the astonishment of his pal standing next to him at the bar, he somehow managed to refill his mug with his own vomit, producing strata of curry colors, a virtual rainbow of gross. His pal turned around to get the attention of another pal to show him what had happened. As they both turned around to see the results of one too many beers, they saw their buddy slam an empty beer mug on the bar. Yes, he did. I know you're in full cringe mode right now because you know what is coming. He downed his own vomit. I mean, he didn't want to waste the alcohol, I guess. This obviously earned him a call sign. He was kind of a big dude, goofy looking and big. So that's where the big comes from. The bird comes from the disgusting eating habits of our feathered

friends. They eat their food and, having loved it so much the first time, they regurgitate their food so they can eat it again. Yummy! So, Big Bird was born and his legendary story lives on.

PITCH: Just a quick clarification. In naval services, a head is where people go to the bathroom. If you know any Marines or sailors, current or former, you may hear them say, "I'm gonna go hit the head." They are not going to hit their head against a wall (even though the military sometimes drives us to want to hit our heads against walls). They are in fact going to the bathroom to relieve themselves. So, a surface warfare officer friend of mine went to a sea warfare school with a Navy F-18 pilot whose call sign was PITCH. On an airplane, pitch is the movement of the aircraft's nose up and down. In this case it meant something different. The F-18 pilot liked to imbibe in various alcoholic beverages from time to time, and when he did he preferred releasing his waters in the ladies' room instead of the men's room. Apparently flight school was a confusing time for him. The F-18 pilot explained to him that PITCH was an acronym that stood for Pisses in the Chick's Head.

LPOD: There was an MH-60S pilot who was about to fly and was taking a ritualistic preflight growler. Everything seemed to go as planned until he went to flush the toilet. Instead of the swirl, he ended up with the explosion. Poo and pee water spread rapidly all over the floor of the head. Desperately, the aviator tried to get out of the stall to get clear of the ensuing flood, but the door, like all bathroom stall doors, opened in instead of out. Opening the door would put him squarely in the path of the poo deluge. So with one foot elevated and the other on the ground, he waited until the flood subsided and exited the disaster area. Unfortunately for someone else, he couldn't stick around to clean up his mess. He had a mission to fly. This earned him the call sign LPOD: Left Poo on Deck.

NAMI WHAMMY

The naval institution for ensuring that naval aviators are physically up to par to fly as aircrew is called NAMI: Naval Aviation Medical Institute. All flight school students fear NAMI. If NAMI finds anything physically disqualifying while you're in flight school, the result is usually dismissal from navy flight training. This is fearfully referred to as the NAMI Whammy. Victims of the NAMI Whammy usually end up as supply officers. Yuck! No whammy, no whammy, no whammy . . .

BRAD: Another MH-60 pilot had a much more embarrassing story. He shat himself immediately after departing from the ship. So BRAD stands for Bowel Release after Departure.

SIMOSS: This one is just gross. I don't even know if I should keep it in, but since I am somehow including you in my inner thought monologue as I write this, here we go. There was a naval flight officer in an F-18 squadron who had way too much to drink the night before a major exercise in Fallon, Nevada. He returned to his BOQ room and commenced to crap all over everything in his room. Montezuma's revenge had nothing on this guy. The walls were covered with high-velocity military-grade poo, as were the bathroom, TV, carpet, and bedsheets. This depraved NFO passed out in this unbelievable disaster and was discovered there, on his poo-spray-covered sheets, covered in his own excrement, by the maids the next morning. Ay Dios Mios! See? Disgusting! SIMOSS (Sea Moss) stands for Sleeps in My Own Shit Spray.

PANDA: The Navy and Marine Corps fly airplanes that are primarily used to fly sailors, Marines, and their families to and fro. They also move generals and admirals to "important" meetings in Thailand and other locales around the world. Among these aircraft is the venerable UC-12W, also known as the B350 KingAir in civilian aviation. A C-12 pilot had flown some general to Clark Air Base in the Philippines, and that night he was out having a pretty good time with his copilot and crew chief on Fields Avenue in Angeles City. There is such a thing as too much of a good time, and this guy's fun meter was definitely pegged. After one too many San Miguels, the C-12 pilot puked his guts out on the street in several high-velocity bursts. Instantly feeling a little more sober, he was ready for round twelve. Since he came from the C-130 community, he didn't already have a call sign. A new call sign was bestowed. Pukes ANd Drinks Again.

SOMOAT: There was a carrier-based F-18 pilot delivering warheads on foreheads over Afghanistan. If you remember Birdbath, he shat on himself twice in the same flight. The unfortunate pilot in this story shat on himself on two separate flights while supporting troops on the ground over Afghanistan. It's bad enough to have done it once, but twice? So SOMOAT stands for Shat on Myself over Afghanistan Twice. I'm sure the good people of Afghanistan are happy that their country's name is used for a call sign memorializing such an impressive performance.

BT: The intelligence officer for one F-35B squadron would have been a pilot himself if he had better eyesight. He's an exception to the rule about who can have a call sign, because his personality was such that he had completely ingratiated himself with the pilots. His sense of humor was on fire, and he was really good at his job. He was not particularly good at international relations. At the Hiroshima Peace Memorial Museum, a mere stone's throw away from where the first atomic weapon ever used in anger detonated, the youngish intelligence officer "trusted a fart" and devastatingly shat himself while in one of the most sacred places in the Japanese consciousness. You might say he dropped a bomb . . . of sorts. It was not easy to hide, either. To make matters worse, when the bomb went off in his pants the sound reverberated through the solemn and sacred confines of the exhibits hall. BT stands for Brown Town, which is a common reference somewhere used to describe the experience of soiling one's self. The call sign itself is not very funny, but I have to chuckle when I picture this Marine officer waddling out of the museum in desperate search of a bathroom where he can clean himself up. You might say Hiroshima got bombed twice. Too soon?

SIS-C (pronounced Sissy): You may remember me mentioning a classy joint in Yuma called Platinum. The finest strippers that Yuma County has to offer dance for dollars there, and the biggest customers are Marines from nearby MCAS Yuma. While on det to Yuma, an MV-22 squadron went out for a night on the town. They drank, ate copious amounts of Mexican food, and topped the night off with a visit to Platinum. As the party was just getting interesting, one aviator was regretting his decision to eat six beef tacos, and he desperately had to go. He had to go bad. He politely asked the stripper to remove herself from his lap and excused himself to the men's room. It was a photo finish poo. His butt barely cleared the bowl before he let loose his blast from the past. As he contemplated how his life had led to him going number two in Yuma's number one strip club, he looked up to discover one of his squadron mates above him with a camera, snapping away to immortalize the event. The picture, him on the toilet giving the photographer the "bird" (yes, I know, the finger, Goose) was used as the "questions" slide for every flight brief for the rest of the time the squadron was in Yuma. He received his new call sign because he Shat in a Strip Club.

The damn thing ain't gonna fix itself. These Marine Corps F-35B mechanics can fix that thing up in a jiffy.

⊨★⊨ SERE SCHOOL POO

SERE school is not a fun place. Over the course of a couple of days, SERE students get put through the wringer in a very realistic training environment. Part of teaching young aviators and snake eaters how to resist their captors is to put them through some light torture and a little something called stress positions. Students spend a night in a small cell that prevents them from moving around a lot, and their only source of relief is a coffee can, where they can sort of roll onto their sides and wee into when nature calls. In the morning, the students all line up with their coffee cans so they can dump the contents therein into a hole in the ground. By this time, you can imagine that the "captive" students are all pretty worn out, having not slept a wink in their cramped cement cells. My buddy Huggy Bear told me of a student in his SERE class who appeared more chipper than the rest. She was a tiny mite of a woman, on the short side of 5'0", and so thin and petite she looked like a strong wind could carry her away. Perhaps her small size allowed her to more comfortably fit into her tiny cubby hole of a cell. Or maybe it was something else. She walked with a slight bounce and a cheerful demeanor to the hole in the ground, emptying the contents of her coffee can in front of all who were present to witness her astonishing accomplishment. All of the other students had poured their coffee cans into the hole with a liquidy swoosh sound, but not the tiny woman in our story. The contents of her can, when emptied into the hole, made a distinct and loud plop-plop sound. So loud that the echo carried a certain amount of gravitas. Somehow she had managed the impossible in her tiny cubby hole cell. Even the instructors, all in character as camp guards, lost their bearing and laughed out loud. Poo is funny.

IPOD: Navy MH-60 pilots are sometimes called upon to conduct VertRep (vertical replenishment) while two ships perform replenishment at sea, or simply RAS. Essentially, a Navy ship will pull alongside a resupply ship, and hoses are "shot" from the supply ship to the Navy ship so thousands of pounds of fuel can be transferred. Cables are "shot" between ships and pallets are winched from the supply ship to the Navy ship with an efficiency and speed that would astound anyone who has never seen RAS before. The 60s hover over the supply ship flight deck and hook up to a sling load, which they then fly to the flight deck of the Navy ship and drop off before going back to the supply ship and doing it all over again and again and again. Fuel, cargo, ammo, aircraft parts, food, office supplies, and mail are all transferred in bulk while two massive ships sail alongside each other in rough seas. All three methods for moving supplies from one ship to the other occur simultaneously, and it is truly something to behold. The MH-60 guys get pretty good at VertRep too. While conducting RAS to an LHD (the smaller helicopter version of an aircraft carrier), a helicopter aircraft commander was about halfway through his VertRep flight when he decided he had to go. We've discussed the piss tube previously. If you remember, the piss tube uses air flow to create suction to dump the urine overboard. This pilot was under the misguided perception that the piss tube led to a plastic bladder that was emptied by the maintenance crew once the flight was over. While his copilot hovered over the deck, and combat cargo Marines struggled to unhook the sling load, the pilot let loose a stream of pee that was sucked out of the aircraft and sprayed all over the poor Marines. IPOD stands for I Pee on Dudes.

GoShow: This call sign was given to an unfortunate MH-60 crew chief. While out flying in the "starboard D," the HAC had to whiz (how many euphemisms can I come up with for poo and pee?). They were still an hour and half away from their next deck hit for fuel. The HAC kindly warned the crew chief that he was about to urinate, which should have been an indication that it was a good time to close the side window and sliding side door. He didn't get the hint. As the HAC commuted his fluids into the briny deep, the piss tube functioned as advertised. The airflow created suction, jettisoning the pee overboard. Unfortunately for the crew chief, there was a small design fault in the piss tube system. The pee tended to spray against the side of the aircraft when leaving the tube, and so it did. The crew chief received an unwanted golden shower from his HAC. He also received a call sign, a rare thing among crew chiefs. In honor of his having received a golden shower, he would forever be known as GoShow.

Flow: Thankfully, this story did not happen to a thirteen-year-old girl. No, this happened to an adult woman who happened to be an NFO in an E/A-18G. Unexpectedly, her time of the month arrived and she was not prepared for the outcome. She bled all over herself and the cockpit, and there was no hiding it. It's nothing to be ashamed of, really. The body does what the body does, and it doesn't do what it does according to your timeline. It's a little embarrassing, though. Naturally, a call sign was bestowed to this NFO. Since her Aunt Flow had come for a visit at a very bad time, she earned the call sign of Flow.

The Mini Boss and the Micro Boss working in the tower, clearing helicopters and jets to launch and recover, holding it down, controlling the chaos.

The commanding officer of the "Green Knights" poses for a shot before a flight off the coast of Subic Bay, Philippines.

CHAPTER 6

CHAPTER 6 | IT'S YOU, IT'S NOT ME

We all have our own idiosyncrasies and traits that make us who we are. Some people's idiosyncrasies and traits are more noticeable than other people's. If you're always angry, selfish, self-absorbed, annoyingly happy ALL THE TIME, or any other personality trait you can think of that comes to define a person's character, you may find yourself with a call sign. The types of idiosyncrasies I'm talking about here are the kind that need only one word, and the person being described suddenly becomes immediately recognized. People also sometimes have physical features that are hard not to notice, or they constantly have a bad odor, or they wear too much perfume; their uniforms may be a little too tight etc., etc., etc. This chapter is the catchall for people in the rarified profession of naval aviation who have a little something special about them that stands out a little too much. It is easy to see the following call signs as mean name-calling. However, I ask that the reader keep in mind that every call sign becomes a term of endearment, no matter how terrible a call sign it might be.

Big boy coming in! An Osprey approaches spot 4 for landing on USS *Wasp*.

Champing at the bits. F-35Bs in the aft slash ready to launch from USS *Wasp*.

☆ GENERAL ORDER #32

"By order of the Base CO: No smoking within 8 hours of flight and no drinking within 50 feet of aircraft."
—Sign posted at a Marine A-4 squadron stationed at Bien Hoa Air Base, South Vietnam

MIAMI: There was an F-35 pilot with some serious issues. He had no time for your issues, whatever they may be, because he was dealing with, like, his own problems, man! Some genius came up with MIAMI for My Issues Are More Important.

ToFu: Common call sign given to pilots and NFOs who have no business strapping into an aircraft or being a naval officer. It stands for Total F**kup. Sometimes guys and gals who get this call sign eventually redeem themselves and figure it all out, but unfortunately for these individuals, the call sign sticks.

Tofu: Like 85 percent of the call signs in this book, a buddy of mine told me about this one. My buddy asked his new squadron mate how he got his call sign, and in a deadpan voice that seemed more to confirm the validity of the call sign rather than express embarrassment, Tofu said, "I'm white and bland."

SLUF: If you've ever seen Tom Cruise in *Top Gun*, it's hard to imagine that there is such a thing as an ugly naval aviator. However, they do exist. Just ask WUNA, SUNA, and NUNA. While it is true that the ugly recipients of those three call signs were all helicopter pilots, and it's probably a little more believable that there are more ugly helicopter pilots than ugly jet guys, the fact remains that ugly is indiscriminate. Some ugly aviators get helicopters and some get jets. Such was the case with an old test pilot who had flown F-14s back in the golden days before the Tailhook scandal. He was short and fat and ugly as sin. You might say he had a face for radio or the kind of face that only a mother could love . . . (maybe!). It's as if he ballooned after being stung by a bee while his face was on fire, and the flames were put out by someone using a pitchfork. His call sign stood for Short Little Ugly F**ker. He was cool with it. Didn't stop him from being a really good pilot.

Fanus: You ever seen someone with a cleft chin that is so distracting you can't see anything else on their face? If that person was a criminal, the one thing you would tell the cops to describe them is that they had a cleft chin that looked like a butt crack. As we all know, the butt crack, if followed to its terminus, leads to the anus. The chin is a facial feature. Combine facial with anus and you get Fanus. Genius! I mean, I suppose Futt Crack would sort of work, too, but I think the better option is Fanus. As it turns out, Fanus is not an uncommon call sign for naval aviators who have been blessed with a defining cleft chin. In recent years, there were two such naval aviators whose careers intersected quite a lot, so much so that when one Fanus was encountered by someone who remembered hearing about a Fanus in a West Coast squadron, the other Fanus would clear up the confusion by stating that he was the East Coast Fanus as opposed to the West Coast Fanus.

FIGJAM: Have you ever encountered one of those guys who tell you how amazing they are? You know the type; they go on and on about all of their accomplishments, how many classes or courses they finished at the top of, or how many women they've seduced. They go on about themselves so much and so often that anyone who has taken a college psychology class or even heard of psychology starts to suspect that maybe this individual has a low self-esteem that they overcompensate for with

Into the sunset. An F-35B launches from the deck of USS *Wasp*.

A Sea Stallion lifts from the deck of USS Wasp at the end of a patrol.

self-aggrandizing word vomit. Maybe this person needs constant external validation to get through the day. What better way to increase someone's self-esteem than to give them a call sign that they will hate? FIGJAM was given to the self-proclaimed top MH-60S pilot in the US Navy. It stands for F**k I'm Good, Just Ask Me.

Phunge: The operations officer of a newly formed MV-22 squadron had formerly been a CH-46E pilot. The CH-46 was a trusty aircraft full of heart and was loved by all who flew and crewed her. The old girl had been around since 1964, and since Boeing sold the manufacturing rights to Mitsubishi, the ones they flew until the very end in 2015 were the same ones they flew in Vietnam in 1965 onward. When I flew God's Chariot we had 46s on our flight line that still had patched up bullet holes courtesy of Victor Charlie. During an overhaul on one particular CH-46E, a mechanic found a Vietnam War–era bullet hole patched with a Budweiser can, cut and hammered flat and puttied to the inside of the airframe. From the front, the 46 sort of looks like a frog. CH-46 crews decided to call it the Frog because Sea Knight, its official name given by Boeing, just doesn't seem to fit. Also, the "f" in frog didn't work for the early CH-46 crews either, so they started calling it the Phrog. Phrog crews spell things with "ph" instead of "f" whenever an f-word is associated with a CH-46. Not that f-word! As the sundown of the world's best helicopter peeked over the horizon, old Phrog pilots started saying Phrogs Phorever at squadron reunions, and while passing each other in hangars now occupied by MV-22s but once occupied by the sexiest aircraft known to have existed. I digress. So back to the OpsO. The dude hated fun. If there was fun in a room and he walked in, the fun just seemed to be sucked up in the vortex of this sinister individual's mind. He was a wet blanket and he knew it. Moreover, he loved being the buzzkill. Early in his career he earned the name Fun Sponge because of his uncanny ability to ruin a good time. His call sign eventually morphed into Funge. Since he was an old Phrog guy, he changed the spelling of his morphed call sign to Phunge. Buzzkiller he may be, mellow harsher through and through, but he still has my respect for remembering his roots and the storied Phrog with the spelling of his call sign. Phrogs Phorever, Phunge, wherever you are.

◗✪◗ THIS STORY WOULD GIVE QUENTIN TARANTINO A NIRALDI!

There are stories that get passed from one generation of student naval aviators (SNA) to the next, and so on and so on. This story is something out of a Quentin Tarantino revenge flick, at least for student naval aviators, because one SNA did what so many of us wanted to do at one point or another in flight school but never had the brass balls to go through with. There was an SNA in primary training, learning the ups and downs of flying the venerable T-34C Turbo Mentor trainer. His "on wing," the instructor pilot (IP) specifically assigned to him, was well known in the squadron as a screamer, or one of the "four horsemen of the apocalypse." You see, each training squadron averages about four IPs who are complete A-holes and who have the highest record for passing out "pink sheets" to students for failing to meet standards. These douche nozzles are known as the four horsemen of the apocalypse, and no student wants to fly with them. In my squadron there was a guy named "Pink Sheet Pete," who was known for failing students at an alarming rate. He was actually a decent dude, but he did have a reputation.

The IP in our story was a raging A-hole. He had the annoying habit of reaching forward in the tandem cockpit from the back seat with his kneeboard and hitting students, or "studs," in the back of the helmet to let them know they screwed up or to add additional pressure during a simulated emergency. The stud in our story was a former Naval Academy lineman, and he was a big dude. During one training flight, after weeks of verbal and quasi-physical abuse from the instructor, the

student was going through the procedures for an engine failure and stumbled over some of the memorized steps. The IP laid into him with the usual verbal abuse, which the student had grown accustomed to. The IP reached forward with his kneeboard and hit the stud in the back of his helmet, this time a little harder than usual, calling him an idiot and adding in a lot of four-letter expletives. This was the straw that broke the camel's back. The SNA wasn't having it. He told the IP over the intercom system (ICS), "You have the controls." Then he called center over the radio and said, "Center, this is Shooter 06; be advised, I am done with this flight and when we get back on the ground I am going to beat the living snot out of my instructor," or something to that effect. Not a word was spoken on the flight home other than the required voice calls to ATC.

Upon landing and shutting down, the stud jumped out of the aircraft and waited for the instructor to unstrap and meet him on the tarmac. This was August in Pensacola. It's hot and humid, to put it mildly. Once the aircraft is shut down, there is no air-conditioning keeping the aircraft cool. The IP stayed strapped in with his canopy closed and waited for rescue, sweating buckets due to the heat and the former lineman pacing outside his cockpit like a tiger. The IP looked straight ahead. Other IPs, having been made aware of the brewing situation, arrived shortly thereafter and calmed the raging student down, escorting him away from the aircraft so the IP wouldn't die of heatstroke sitting in the hot cockpit or otherwise be bludgeoned to death by the student's massive

F-35B pilot mounting his mighty steed

Looking like space ships, two F-35Bs are silhouetted by the dawn off the coast of the Philippines on board USS *Wasp*.

Portrait of a SAR pilot on board USS America

fists. The stud was grounded for a while, but eventually he continued in flight school and later earned his wings. The IP was also grounded and given a reprimand because other SNAs came forward and said they had similar run-ins with the instructor calling them names and hitting them in the back of the helmet with his kneeboard. I have no doubt the stud felt vindicated, and whatever the punishment he received he probably thought it was well worth it.

Postscript to the above story: When I finished flight school I was sent to Camp Pendleton to learn how to fly the CH-46E at the RAG, HMM-164(T) "Knightriders." Legend has it that the CO of that squadron when I was there was the same SNA who, while in flight school, threatened to kick his IP's butt. When this CO was motivated about something, he would say, "That gives me a niraldi!" No one knew what that meant, so one day during a squadron formation someone asked him. The skipper said, "It's a full-body erection!"

TOTY: A Marine F/A-18D pilot really put the work in while he was going through the F-18 RAG on the West Coast. He absolutely crushed all of his events and scored the highest-average grades among his peers. Due to his hard work and excellent flying abilities, he was selected as the Student of the Year. When he reached his fleet squadron in Beaufort, South Carolina, his squadron mates weren't impressed. To them, he was just Nick the new guy, a nugget who didn't know the first thing about flying in the fleet. He still had to earn his stripes just like the rest of them. So naturally, instead of congratulating the Student of the Year for his accomplishment, they made fun of him for it. They unofficially gave him the call sign POTY, which sneeringly stood for Pilot of the Year and of course was a poo joke (yes, that is in fact the level of maturity we're dealing with here). That call sign, however, did not last. One day, he gave his squadron mates all the material they would need to assign him his permanent call sign. He was given the task of conducting engine run-ups for an aircraft coming out of phase maintenance. This included running up the engines in the chocks with the brakes engaged, followed by a high-speed run down the runway. As a reward for hard work, a maintainer was selected to ride in the back seat for a little thrill ride, and oh what a ride he got! So off they went, roaring down the runway at high speed, reaching 120 knots. As they approached the high-speed turnoff taxiway, the pilot hit the brakes and turned the aircraft to the left, exiting the runway. As the jet careened around the curve, the brakes on the left landing gear seized up due to overheating, and the left tires blew out. It was a hot day in Beaufort, and the brakes were already hot from all the engine run-ups in the chocks. After wrestling the aircraft to a standstill and shutting down the engines, the aircraft came to rest in the middle of the taxiway and would taxi no farther. It just wasn't his day! It should be noted that anything stupid this guy did got him some nickname that ended with "of the Year." When he messed up taxiing back to the flight line so bad, it was only natural that they would stick with the theme. His call sign (this one stuck) was changed to Taxi of the Year. It's amazing that his worthy accomplishment of being the best at the RAG would follow him for the rest of his career in the form of a call sign that made fun of his taxiing abilities. No good deed goes unpunished, apparently.

Bus: This one is short and to the point. A dude had the last name of Short (see what I did there?)

IKIA: IKEA is the Swedish furniture superstore, which sells cheap furniture with ridiculously difficult assembly instructions. It's the kind of furniture that is nice to look at but doesn't last. A UH-1Y pilot, who had recently returned from a tour in Afghanistan before checking in to his new squadron, was just a little too salty for some of the Cobra WTIs. He had a tendency to question them whenever he felt their information was suspect. There was one particular incident that earned our Huey pilot the

F-35B fighter pilot

ire of the Cobra WTIs. One day while walking through the hallways of his squadron spaces, a Cobra WTI approached the young Huey pilot and attempted to quiz him on his knowledge about enemy weapons engagement zones. The skid community had recently witnessed two midair collisions resulting from Cobras running into other aircraft. Our hero responded to the pop quiz with "I don't give a darn about the weapons engagement zones because I am far more likely to die by having you run into me than by being hit by a surface-to-air missile." At his squadron's Cobra court, his call sign was changed from "Zeeb" (not a very funny story) to IKIA, because the WTIs said he was cheap and flimsy, like the famous Swedish furniture. This was more of a dig at his weapons and tactics knowledge, which he used to challenge the WTIs, than it was against his character. IKIA stands for "I Know It All." WTIs are notorious for being know-it-alls. The hypocrisy of this call sign is so thick you could stick a straw in it and call it a milkshake.

Zika: Remember the Zika virus? It was cool way before COVID-19 was cool. Imagine a Cobra pilot with a big body (tall and thick boned) but with a small head that doesn't seem to fit his robust figure. Little head, big body . . . like the Zika virus.

Centa: Some people are just not attractive. This guy, a Marine MV-22 pilot, was ugly as sin. He was so ugly that his squadron mates thought maybe his parents had mistakenly thrown out the baby and kept the placenta. Centa is short for placenta. I'm sure he had a great personality though!

✈ THE ITALIAN STUDENT AND THE CASE OF THE MIDAIR SEAT SWAP

Solo flights in flight school are always flown from the front seat of the tandem-seat training aircraft. One day, a student naval aviator with a thick Italian accent checked in to the Navy Outlying Field in Brewton, Alabama. The Italian Navy SNA said, "Barootin, F-ah D-O, this is a Shooter 16 Solo, for landing." As he made his short final, the field duty officer noticed that the solo student was flying from the back seat. "Shooter 16 Solo! You're supposed to be in the front seat!" After making his touch-and-go landing, the Italian solo came on the radio, saying, "Me scuzzi! I sweetch!" As he came back in for his second landing after going around the landing pattern, the FDO was shocked to see the solo pilot flying from the front seat. The FDO was speechless. Somehow the Italian Navy solo pilot had climbed out onto the wing and moved from the rear cockpit to the front cockpit midflight. "Okay, I am in a the front seat a now!" What the FDO didn't know was that the Italian Navy SNA wasn't solo at all. The instructor pilot in the back had the Italian Navy student scrunch down in the front so he couldn't be seen, and then had the Italian student make the radio calls. On the next pass, the instructor scrunched down and the student popped up, giving the impression that the "solo" student had switched from the back to the front cockpit in midflight. I bet the former FDO, who has long since moved on, still tells that story in stunned amazement, still believing that the Italian Navy SNA sweetched seats midflight.

Spectrum: Every squadron in naval aviation has at least one guy who is "Rain Man" smart. He's great with numbers, can write wicked code to make an Excel spreadsheet do unimaginable things, and can recite every line from the *Lord of the Rings* trilogy. We had a guy whose call sign was Beaker because he sort of meeped out his words and was wicked smart like Beaker from the Muppets. There's a mental condition for this known as Asperger's, wherein you have a highly capable and intelligent person who has absolutely zero social skills and usually has some sort of tick they use to calm themselves down. If you have Asperger's you are on the autism spectrum. So, either this particular Cobra

pilot had Asperger's or he was on the complete opposite side of the spectrum and had straight-up ADHD and couldn't pay attention to anything or focus on anything unless he was hyperfocused on it. Either way, it was assumed by his squadron mates that he was somewhere on the spectrum. Since I received this call sign story directly from Spectrum himself via email, I cannot confirm which side of the spectrum he was on.

Mavwick: An MH-53 pilot had the last name of Wick. He also had a slight speech impediment. He pronounced his Rs with a slight W sound, so the combination of his last name with his speech impediment gives us this subtle but brilliant example of a call sign.

Maverick: Let it be known that I have searched far and wide for a naval aviator or NFO with the call sign of Maverick. I knew that this call sign, if I ever found it, would be given only to someone with the mean-spirited-term-of-endearment principle in mind. I was not disappointed. A naval flight officer in a Navy Prowler squadron was not very good at his job or at being an officer in general. Many call signs were offered, but each one generated a complaint to the squadron commanding officer, and each was shot down. This particular NFO kept a diary of all slights, perceived or otherwise, and was very sensitive in an environment that doesn't much care for sensitivity. In other words, he didn't understand the program. So his squadron mates eventually settled on Maverick. Maverick wore that call sign as a badge of honor, failing to recognize that it was given for the exact opposite reason this person thought it was given to them for. Maverick was a tongue-in-cheek call sign. Very tongue in cheek.

Speed Bag: Given to an E-2 pilot who had the kind of face you just wanted to punch

Dudeboat: An F-18 pilot had the last name of Manship. Dudeboat Manship.

Porta-john: Another guy named Wick sort of looked like a sickly, less attractive Keanu Reeves, who played John Wick in several movies of the same name. Essentially, this F-18 pilot looked like a Shitty John Wick.

Dog Balls: Call signs don't always make sense. At a Hail and Farewell, the squadron XO had a little too much to drink. In the Navy the squadrons will sometimes give new guys a temporary call sign until they do something stupid and earn their permanent one. When the first new guy stepped up, the pilots started throwing out call sign suggestions. The XO suddenly blurted out, "Dog Balls!" The name stuck. It instantly became the young pilot's permanent call sign. Apparently the XO had always wanted to bestow that unfortunate moniker upon someone.

Annie: A Navy MH-60S pilot grew up an orphan and was passed from foster home to foster home. He made good, though, went to college, commissioned in the Navy, and became a pilot. One day while on deployment he got into an argument over an ethical issue with his roommate on the ship. The argument was pretty heated, whatever it was about. At one point the foster kid who made good responded to his roommate's argument by yelling, "That's not how I was raised!," to which his roommate responded with "What, without parents?!" A low blow to be sure. They made up and stayed friends, but the foster kid got a new call sign. He was the little orphan "Annie."

PI (pronounced Pie): In the world of aviation, the maintenance required for aircraft would astound the layman. For instance, the MV-22B requires 100 man-hours of maintenance for every single hour of flight time. When an aircraft breaks or reaches a certain time limit that requires what is called a

Green deck! An F-35B flashes past on board USS *America*.

phased maintenance period (going into phase), everything that was adjusted, fixed, updated, or otherwise modified must be tested before the aircraft can be put out on the flight line for operations and training flights. The pilots who conduct the test flights are called functional check pilots (FCPs), and they usually tend to be book smart as well as people who can handle an aircraft well. PI was a graduate of Princeton University who was living the dream as a Marine F-18 pilot. He was wicked smart and the best FCP in the squadron, if not the wing. There was a downside. He was a social moron. I don't mean to say he didn't know how to tell a joke. I mean any interaction with PI was bound to be awkward. On the spectrum of autism, he would probably fall out as someone with Asperger's. Give him anything technically complicated or any problem too difficult for the mortal man's brain, and like Rainman he will just figure it out with little to no thought. If you told him a joke or introduced him to a woman, you'd better standby for serious stone-faced awkwardness. PI stands for Princeton Idiot.

Shop Vac / Roomba: There was an MH-60B pilot who was very loud and sucked at life. So he received the call sign Shop Vac. Makes sense. When he became self-aware that he was loud and sucked at life, his call sign was changed to Roomba.

Thug: Everyone has a breaking point. There was a Marine F-18 pilot who was the most mild-mannered dude in the fleet. He was quiet and unassuming and preferred to be left alone. One might even describe him as meek. You might be thinking that he received Thug as some sort of ironic call sign, but you would be wrong to assume that. While at SERE school he was being slapped around by one of the SERE instructors, who was acting within the bounds of his job description in trying to prepare students for the unfortunate possibility of falling into enemy hands. Mr. Meek wasn't having it. The quiet and unassuming F-18 pilot head-butted the instructor right in the nose, breaking it and sending the instructor to the hospital. It's always the quiet ones you have to worry about.

GAMES WE LIKE TO PLAY

There are little games we play with the guys who ride in the backs of our helicopters. On the Phrog, for instance, there was a hand pump near the ramp on the back end of the cabin that was used to either manually raise and lower the ramp or prime the hydraulic pump to do it with a lever. So, the trick was to convince the grunts that something had gone horribly wrong with the aircraft. To do this, the pilots would start showing signs of distress, while wiggling the sticks in order to make the ride a little bumpy. At some point the pilots would start descending, and the crew chief would rush to the back of the cabin to start pumping the hand pump, as though it had anything at all to do with flying straight and level in an emergency. Pretending that the pilots needed him up front, the crew chief would assign one of the poor grunts to start pumping. When the grunt pumped, the aircraft would start to climb. When the grunt got tired and started slowing down, the aircraft would descend again. The crew chief would tell the pilots when to climb and when to descend. So the grunts in back would start cycling guys in; each would take a turn until they were worn out and dripping with sweat. Just a little joke. Another fun little game was getting a grunt to pee on himself. If one of the grunts in back ever had to go pee while in flight, some unscrupulous crew chiefs would tell him to just pee off the back of the ramp. The problem with that is there is an aerodynamic oddity just off the ramp wherein the wind blows into the cabin instead of out of it, even though the aircraft is flying forward. So if you relieved yourself off the ramp, you essentially pissed into the wind and all over yourself. I wonder why the grunts didn't like us air wingers. I guess we're kind of A-holes, huh?

T-Rex: We all know that the T. rex had short arms. The real danger of the T. rex was its massive thighs and its really big mouth bristling with sharp teeth. So just keep that image in your head while I tell you about a C-130 pilot who was called T-Rex. When it came time to pay for drinks, dinner, soda, etc., this guy always came up short with the money. He always scammed his way out of paying for anything when food or booze was involved. Night out on the town? Time to pay up? T-Rex is in the bathroom. Essentially his arms were too short, like a T. rex's arms, to reach his wallet. Additionally, he had one hell of a mouth on him and could insult anyone with his rapier British-like sense of humor. His verbal assaults were akin to being figuratively attacked by a T. rex.

T-Rex: Well, yes, there's more than one. A CH-53E pilot had really short arms. She was also an avid Crossfit nut, and she could take down anyone with her ability to put people in their place with a good old-fashioned dressing down. So, she had small arms and was a man-eater. It seemed to fit. The best part was what her squadron mates would do with this call sign. When she walked by them in the hallways of their squadron spaces, they would freeze in place, like they did in *Jurassic Park*, so the T-Rex wouldn't know that they were there. If there was a glass of water on a table or desk when she walked into a room or office, they would hit the table so the water would do that ripple thing it did in the movie when the T. rex was approaching. She was a good sport about it. She just called them pricks and went about her day.

Feel the speed. An F-35B conducts a flyby for the crew of USS *Wasp*.

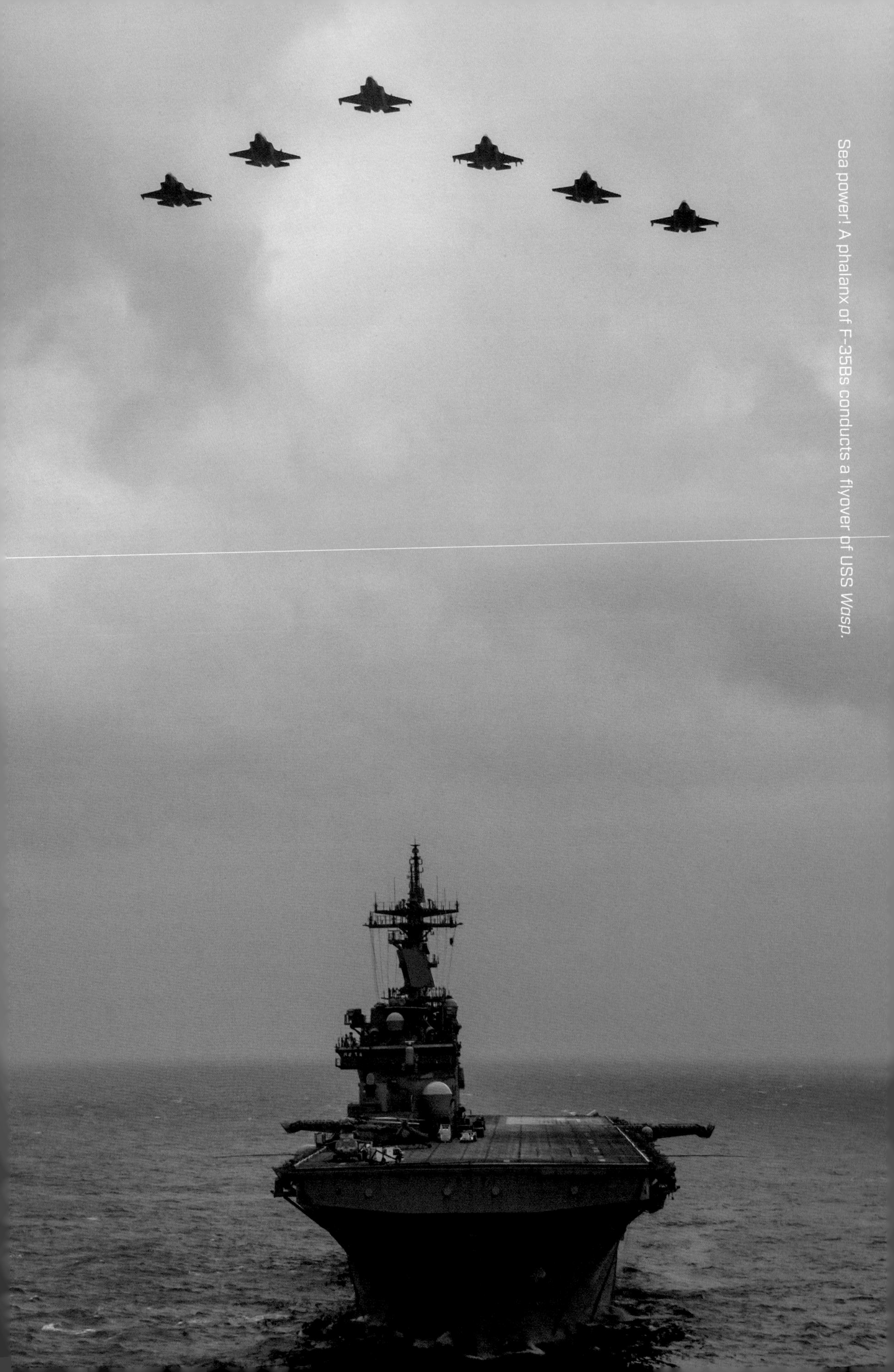

Sea power! A phalanx of F-35Bs conducts a flyover of USS *Wasp*.

Rudy: Have you seen this inspirational movie about a kid with zero athletic ability but lots of heart who gets to suit up at the end and run for a touchdown for Notre Dame? Great movie, right? Complete BS, though. Turns out the guy the movie was about was a bit of a fraudster and made the story up. One MH-60S pilot hated, nay, loathed this movie. He pegged Rudy as a "try-hard" and a fraud and was obsessed with his hatred of the movie. He was no fun to watch *Rudy* with. Fast forward to the kangaroo court. The CO asked if there were any call sign recommendations for the pilot in our story, and everyone yelled in unison, "Rudy!"

Spork: Tools have many uses. Sometimes you have the wrong tool for the job, but it sort of works. You can use an ax as a hammer, or a screwdriver to cut into something. So when an MH-60S pilot turned out to be both a jerk and only semi-useful, a call sign was born. A spork is not the best tool for eating. As a spoon it's practically useless, and the prongs aren't long enough to grab a piece of food. It works, but just barely. In other words, it's not the tool you want, but it's the tool you have, just like the guy whose call sign is Spork.

HAMtrak: This one is sort of a mix between a play on words, an acronym, and a general description of the effects of alcohol on one female MV-22B pilot. Young and attractive, she was a competent pilot and officer in her squadron. When out for a night of boozing with squadron mates, she was known to get a little too big for her alcohol britches. She tended to leave a path of destruction like a train wreck and was usually the only one who didn't remember what happened after the smoke cleared. HAM stands for Hot-Ass Mess, and the trak part addresses the train wreck nature of her occasional big nights. HAMtrak, pronounced like Amtrak with an H, was a Hot-Ass Mess who drinks until she goes off the rails. Like an Amtrak train wreck, you just can't look away.

Donny: You remember Donny from a previous call sign story about an AH-1W pilot with the call sign of Trunchbull. Donny was the name of the character played by Steve Buscemi in the movie *The Big Lebowski*. The Donny I knew was always "running his suck" about stuff he knew little about, but somehow he sounded like the subject matter expert. This can create problems during planning, because if you don't verify Donny's information you may end up holding the bag when the information turns out to be wrong. People had gotten used to this, so whenever he chimed in, everybody told him to "Shut the f**k up, Donny! You're in over your head." Good dude, though.

⬟⭐ SPEAKING OF *THE BIG LEBOWSKI* . . .

When I was on my first at-sea deployment, *The Big Lebowski* was a big movie for my squadron. We were always quoting the movie. It didn't matter where we were. "Tiger 12, 13, return to base," to which Tiger 13 would reply, "The Dude abides." We incorporated movie quotes and references in briefs and regular conversation. People outside the squadron grew tired of the bad Dude impersonations. On the ship there is a tower where the air boss (think *Top Gun*) provides control to aircraft within the ship's 5-mile radius. The mini boss is usually up there as well. In addition, the embarked squadron provides a pilot in the tower to serve as the squadron rep. This guy is referred to as the "Tower Flower," or simply "flower." With the squadron CO's permission we changed the name of the Tower Flower to "Dude." It was cool because we could legitimately say dude on the radio. Good times! Years later, I was working in the tower on USS *Wasp*. USS *Essex* had long before returned to the States for a two-year yard period, and *Wasp* was working in its place. A CH-53 pilot who was filling in as the tower flower on *Wasp* told me that when he was on *Essex* six years after my squadron had sullied her flight deck, the tower flower was still being called "Dude." It warmed my heart.

An F-35B in afterburner flies low over USS *Wasp*.

MOOOP: There was this guy in my squadron who was some sort of Zen master or something. He always looked so serene and contemplative. He was different because he had attended the Merchant Marine Academy instead of THE academy (Which one?). He definitely marched to the smell of his own patchouli stink. He was a good dude (lots of good dudes in naval aviation), but he was not the usual personality type you find in the meat-eater community of combat pilots. The squadron was doing an exercise in the Philippines, and the CO wanted well-done squadron photos to capture his time as a squadron commander. I guess he wanted to remember us. One of the photos was of all the officers in the squadron, standing in front of two CH-46s parked nose to nose. In the back row was the Zen master looking up at the clouds passing by instead of at the camera. He was a Marine Officer on Own Program.

WILCO: This is a radio term that stands for Will Comply. In one particular MH-60S squadron there was a pilot who was so happy and so energetic that her squadron mates became convinced she was constantly on cocaine (she wasn't). Her call sign was WILCO, which stands for Wow I Love COcaine.

MAW: An F-14 pilot had a constant look of illness about him. He was skinny, pale, and very young looking. The other pilots thought he was on the verge of death and that he could have been a candidate for the Make-A-Wish Foundation. MAW . . . Make a Wish.

⊱✪⊰ SOUND ADVICE

Eat what the monkey eats, then eat the monkey.
　　—instruction given at the basic land survival course for student naval aviators

PAM: I knew an MH-60S pilot who was bright and bubbly and seemed to always need attention from her fellow aviators. She had an adorable personality and everyone liked her, but she reminded everyone of a puppy that just wanted to be the center of your attention. PAM stands for Pay Attention to Me.

TUBA: A brand-new AH-1W pilot showed up to his squadron, and he had gained a little weight since having started flight school. The flight suits he was issued in Pensacola were all just a little too tight on him. TUBA stands for Tight Uniform, Big Ass.

WUNA: A bit overused, but still funny. World's Ugliest Naval Aviator. There are other variations. World's Angriest Naval Aviator, World's Youngest Naval Aviator . . . you get the point. You can also change the locality. For instance, there was a guy at Marine Corps Air Station New River in North Carolina who was known as NUNA, for New River's Ugliest Naval Aviator.

BARF: Have you ever seen those big farmer boys, corn fed, allergic to the sun? You know those guys? Well, there was an E-2C Hawkeye pilot who had a big rear end, which sort of moved independently of the rest of his body, and a big ugly red face. Of course BARF works to describe those blessed with lovely personalities but not so blessed in looks. As you can tell, BARF is spelled in all caps, so it's an acronym. Big Ass Red Face.

LAMCHOP: A buddy of mine went to flight school with a Navy guy who, like my buddy, eventually became an F-18 pilot. That community is not very big, and F-18 pilots both from the Marines and the Navy all tend to know each other. This Navy guy was a little short. So naturally he was made fun of. I know that sounds mean, but this isn't elementary school . . . okay, some of the humor is elemental, but we don't do it to bully or demean. We do it out of love. In naval aviation it's all part of the camaraderie associated with people who do a dangerous job together. The sooner you come to terms with this, the more fun it will be for you. So this guy earned his call sign because he was not a quick study of "We're just messing with you, and you need to roll with it" game plan, and his little-man Napoleon complex didn't help. He took the ribbing very personally and then threw temper tantrums. For instance, when his squadron mates painted "NO STEP" on top of his flight helmet, he lost his temper. For the sake of clarification, there are certain *sensitive* spots on aircraft that should not be stepped on, and these spots are marked by the painted-on words "NO STEP." Look out your window at the top of the wing the next time you fly the friendly skies, and you'll see what I'm going on about. This guy also didn't like it when the tallest plane captain offered to give him a boost to help him get his foot up to the first rung of the boarding ladder. He also hated when his fellow aviators delighted in running his seat to the bottom detent and adjusting the foot pedals all the way forward just to watch his reaction when he got in the jet. He was the Little Angry Man who Can't Handle Our Program.

SUNA: Apparently, WUNA was already taken by another pilot in the squadron. So this guy was the Second Ugliest Naval Aviator.

An F-35B hovers to a landing on spot 9 on board USS *America*.

LOIS: An E-2C pilot didn't like people making fun of him. He was no different than any other naval aviator. There was nothing in particular that stood out about him for people to make fun of, so the jokes were really just the run-of-the-mill kidding that all naval aviators endure. He didn't like it at all. You might say he was overly sensitive. LOIS stands for Lay Off, I'm Sensitive!

Ring: An E-2C NFO had the defining characteristic of being an A-hole when he didn't like what he saw. Whether as an XO of a squadron or an instructor in the back of a Hawkeye, if you screwed up in his presence he really let you have it. His last name was Browning. Another name for the anus is Brown Ring. Now you get it.

Shirt Pocket: As in, as useless as a Shirt Pocket. This was bestowed to a JO in a helicopter squadron who was having a really hard time meeting the standard.

Treich (Trike): It should be noted that controversial call signs should always have two stories: the one that is true, and the one you tell your mom. When Tom Cruise began work on *Top Gun II: Maverick*, he asked for the Navy's full cooperation in producing the film. Because of this cooperation, many actual TOPGUN instructors appear in *Top Gun II*. In the first *Top Gun* film, the pilots and NFOs who contributed to the film were given credit for their efforts in the end-credits scene, and their call signs were included in their listed names. Tom Cruise wanted the same for *Top Gun II*, but the Navy's air boss (chief of Naval Air Forces) wanted the list of call signs submitted for his review, because heaven forbid an offensive call sign should be seen in the end credits; the pristine nature of naval aviators that the Department of the Navy wishes to promote may have been besmirched if this was to happen. In the end, no contributing Navy pilots had their call signs listed in the end credits, lest someone should ask a question as to what one or two of the call signs meant. Treich, in particular, was suspiciously suspicious. The air boss asked for an explanation, and the TOPGUN commander gave him the real story instead of the made-up one. The pilot who bore this call sign was muscular, broad shouldered, 6'3" tall, blond haired, blue eyed, square jawed, and handsome. Someone in his first fleet squadron exclaimed that he looked like the poster child for the Third Reich. This was the explanation provided to the air boss. Now remember, call signs are never flattering. They are demeaning and mean spirited, so calling this guy a Nazi was meant as an insult to a ridiculously good-looking dude who was definitely "kein Nazi." The air boss didn't see it that way. He demanded that the call sign be scrubbed immediately, and that a new call sign be given. Probably for the best. There may be some people out there who don't understand how call signs work, and they may get their feelings hurt. Alas . . .

Chainsaw: A Marine EA-6B Prowler NFO was a bit too loud and obnoxious for his fellow squadron mates. He was also a very simple fellow. In other words, he was a loud and obnoxious tool.

LOTHAR: The Brits don't know this, because they think they're better than we are, but they are much more like us than they like to believe. We are in fact Britain's spawn, historically speaking. The USA is essentially the child that grew up and was more successful than their dad. We make fun of people, just like they do, to show our affection. The Brits may have an edge on us with their rapier wit, and American women definitely love their accents, but nevertheless we won our war of independence and they failed to keep us within the realm. We joke and chide, but in the end, American naval aviators tend to work very well with their counterparts from across the pond. In fact, there are exchange programs where the Brits will send select pilots to fly in our squadrons for a couple of years, and we'll send select pilots to fly in their squadrons for a couple of years. The only difference is that the Brits are already alcoholics when they show up to the American squadrons, whereas the American pilots become alcoholics by the time they leave the British squadrons. LOTHAR is a common call sign given to Brits when they come over on exchange. It stands for Loser of THe American Revolution. It's not very original or clever, but there you go. One such LOTHAR went to a Navy Super Hornet squadron at NAS Lemoore and was the first-ever British exchange pilot to be selected to go to TOPGUN. This was such a big deal that it raised an eyebrow or two across the pond, and the British Sea Lord had to brief this momentous occasion to the Queen herself. Unfortunately, the Sea Lord told the Queen the real story behind LOTHAR, and she was not well pleased. Queen Elizabeth II's third-great-grandfather, after all, was King George III, who was king when the colonials threw the tea into Boston Harbor, and in 1783, when the United States won its independence. Perhaps she was being overly sensitive, but nevertheless LOTHAR's call sign created a bit of a diplomatic row between the United States and Great Britain. Too soon?

IAD . . . S (pronounced Eye-ads): We all know people who have mouths that will run forever. Long after the brain goes dead, the jaw will just keep working, as if there is so much BS that still needs to be said. These guys tend to be silver tongued and sharp witted. They say things to get others to react, often in negative ways, and they relish in pissing people off with their vitriolic verbal vomit. There was an F-18 NFO from South Philly who had a smarmy South Philly accent to go along with his searing tongue and loud mouth. He was such a douchebag that he gladly acknowledged it, telling people that it was how he showed love. He was commonly overheard telling people, I Am a Douche . . . Seriously (IAD . . . S). IADS in military terms is the acronym for Integrated Air Defense System, which is essentially a country's planned defense against aerial attack and the weapons, command and control, and detection equipment they have to defend a target area. As such, this acronym makes sense to pilots who may one day get the call to fly into a target area with an Integrated Air Defense System. Psychologists would probably equate a loud mouth's behavior as a sort of defensive mechanism based on the loud mouth's insecurities. I can see that. Maybe that's what makes this call sign so applicable. IAD . . . S used his humor and South Philly attitude as a defense against "aerial attack" from smart-mouthed, sophomoric squadron mates.

Shithead: There was a Navy MH-53 pilot who was a bit of *scheizekopf*. He just kept making mistakes, blaming others, showing up late for flight briefs, hitting on other pilots' wives, and other general craptastic activities. There is an obvious problem with Shithead; you can't say that over the radio. It's a rule. To get around this obstruction of justice, his squadron mates simply pronounced shithead as Shith-ead. What a crappy call sign! *Author's note*: MH-53 pilots don't usually get call signs, so . . .

FUN FACT

In the United Kingdom they like to drink. Okay, that's well known. What isn't well known is that sometimes they play a drinking game called "Top Gin," a play on the movie title *Top Gun* (this is why this is related to naval aviation). While watching *Top Gun*, everyone has a glass of gin. Each player draws several pieces of paper from a hat. Each time something appears in the movie that matches what is written on a piece of paper, whoever has that piece of paper has to drink. Say you have a piece of paper that has the phrase "high five" on it, then you have to drink every time someone on screen does a high five. If another of your pieces of paper has the word "sunglasses" on it, you must drink every time someone is wearing sunglasses in the film. It gets out of hand very quickly. Take small sips.

An F-35B pilot poses for a portrait on board USS *America*.

Syndrome: This one made me blow milk through my nose. Laugh-out-loud funny and just plain terrible. I am a little ashamed that it made me laugh so hard, but it was instantaneous and unstoppable. I simply could not control myself. There was an EA-6B pilot who looked like she was special; special in a Down syndrome sort of way.

Bjorn: There's a company called Bjorn that makes safety products for babies. They make car seats, strollers, milk bottles, etc. They also make baby carriers. You know those carriers you wear on your chest with your little crumb-snatcher just bobbing their little head around, slobbering all over their meaty little hands and rubbing it all over your face? So there was this MV-22B pilot who was just above the threshold for dwarfism. He would be considered tall in Munchkinville but would be average height in the ball pit at Chuck E. Cheese's. Someone brought a modified C-bag to the squadron kangaroo court, having cut leg holes out of the bottom. With help from his willing squadron mates, this Schmuckatelli lifted the not-a-midget naval aviator into the C-bag with his legs going through the holes, and then carried the little guy around the K-court as if he was carrying his own kid. As it turns out, the not-a-midget was bobbing his head around and slobbering all over his meaty little hands just like a real baby. Alcohol is a hell of a drug! They were both drunk and had a great time. Right there on the spot you have a fully grown man (not as full grown as others) being carried in a tactical baby carrier; it was an instant call sign assignment. There's an MV-22 pilot out there barely tall enough to ride Thunder Mountain at Disneyland whose call sign is Bjorn.

Fetus: A guy in my squadron was short and so young looking that he gave off a baby vibe. One of the squadron wives said they wanted to hold him and rock him to sleep. He was a good friend of mine and definitely a good dude, but he had this very condescending way about him. He wasn't

Namaste on USS *America*

condescending; it was just his intonation when speaking. He was our squadron S6 guy, essentially the IT guy. He was good with computers. There's this skit that used to be on *Saturday Night Live* back in the days of Jimmy Fallon and Tina Fey. It was about an IT guy (Fallon) who would fix people's computers but make them feel stupid because they couldn't perform simple troubleshooting tasks. "Did you try restarting it?" Jimmy Fallon would ask and in frustration tell the person to "MOVE!" so he could fix whatever the stupid problem was. That character was the *Saturday Night Live* embodiment of my pal Fetus. Imagine this little dude with the funny baby-like hair who looks like he should still be getting his diaper changed telling you in the most condescending way possible how to fix your computer. You can't call a guy baby, so the call sign gods went with the next best thing.

FUNGUS: A new guy showed up to a CH-46E squadron. His only sin in this instance was being Nick the new guy. As such, he received one of the worst call signs of all time: F U New Guy U Suck.

GLIB: The *Oxford English Dictionary* definition for sycophant is as follows: a person who praises important or powerful people too much and in a way that is not sincere, especially in order to get something from them. The commanding officer of a Navy F-18 squadron had the call sign Ghost. It sounds cool, but I am sure there is an embarrassing story behind it. In this squadron there was a young lieutenant who put an inordinate amount of effort into winning Ghost's favor. This is sometimes an occurrence between the powerful and the wannabe powerful. The young lieutenant was a butt kisser who would do anything to win the love of his CO, and his fellow JOs called him on it. GLIB stands for Ghost's Little Insignificant Bitch. You reap what you sow.

Stall horn: On airplanes there is a warning system that tells you when you are approaching stall speed. If an airplane slows down too much while flying, the wings will stop producing usable lift, which can cause the aircraft to depart controlled flight. The stall horn is very annoying, by design, so that the pilot immediately recognizes the situation and makes corrections to avoid stalling out. A Navy helicopter pilot had a very annoying voice, which echoed down the hallways of squadron spaces warning you of his imminent arrival. You get it. (*Note*: helicopters don't have stall horns, so . . .)

SMINAH: There's this thing called anthropomorphic measuring, wherein a potential pilot is measured to see if they will fit into the aircraft that are currently used by the Navy and Marine Corps, and whether or not they will be able to reach all of the buttons and knobs. There was once a young captain who earned her wings at jet school, only to discover that she couldn't reach all the buttons and doodads in the cockpit when she showed up to the F-18 RAG at Miramar. Most importantly, she couldn't reach the overhead ejection handle. Not good! Somehow she slipped through the cracks and never should have been sent to jet school, on the basis of her original anthropomorphic measurements. Once the doctors re-measured her and determined that her arms were too short for jets, she was sent to helicopter school to requalify as a helo pilot. I'm sure she thrived with her T. rex–like arms in whatever helicopter she selected for. Her call sign was "Bubbles," but I don't know why. The point of the above story is that sometimes people slip through the cracks of the very thorough medical-screening process that student naval aviators go through before they're allowed to wiggle the sticks of a multimillion-dollar aircraft. For instance, there was a guy who somehow made it into flight school, got his wings, and ended up a Huey pilot on the West Coast. Everyone was convinced that he was an actual midget. They were convinced that somehow he had skipped the anthropomorphic-measurement process, and no one ever noticed. So they called him SMINAH . . . Shortest Man in Naval Aviation History.

TACO: There was a woman who flew MH-60Rs who would not stop talking. This woman, unfortunately, had the gift of gab. Most of what she talked about were complaints about her girlfriends, complaints about her mom, complaints about the CO, complaints about work, complaints about the Navy, complaints about it being too sunny on sunny days and too rainy on rainy days. TACO stands for Talks Always, Complains Often.

FUPA: I'm not super familiar with the slang the kids are using these days, but apparently this stands for Fat Upper Private Area. I am not here to body-shame, but there are people who have an excess amount of fat around the area between their junk and their belly buttons, which is sort of an extension of their nether region. This excess fat tends to jiggle around a bit, and the bearer of a FUPA usually has to do some trick with their belt and trousers to keep it in place. It's hard to imagine that a Marine EA-6B pilot who is expected to maintain his physique would allow himself to expand to the point of having a minor FUPA. It made him look really funny in a flight suit.

SCRAT: You know that little prehistoric squirrel from the animated classic *Ice Age* that's always trying to get a nut that somehow always seems to stay just out of reach? That little dude's name was Scrat. The unfortunate MH-60S pilot who earned this name did so by contracting testicular cancer and ending up with one less ball to play with during "me time." I guess that was the price he was willing to pay to survive cancer. So SCRAT is a very apropos name in that Scrat the squirrel lost a nut and couldn't seem to get it back, just like SCRAT. You get it. SCRAT of course is an acronym for Survived Cancer, Removed a Testicle. According to the people who know him, SCRAT kind of resembles Scrat, so it's a call sign with several layers.

IRA: A wee lad from the Emerald Island came to America with his ma and pa to escape "the Troubles." He eventually became your typical American boy who talked like an Irishman but loved baseball and football like a red-blooded 'merican. His family was connected to the Irish Republican Army, an important player in "the Troubles," so his call sign (pronounced like the popular Yiddish name of old) literally stands for Irish Republican Army.

BOMB: CH-53E pilots and MH-53E pilots are a special breed. Seriously, they aren't quite human. They're more humanoid than human. Ever seen an old 1980s movie called *CHUD: Cannibalistic Humanoid Underground Dwellers*? They're sort of like that but they don't live underground, and as far as anyone knows they aren't cannibals. There was one Neanderthal-looking dude who breathed through his open mouth more often than not. He was a big country boy from Dirtwad, Texas. He enjoyed soft porn, chewing tobacco, and talking about how much weight he could lift with one arm. One arm was larger than the other, but it wasn't because he was lifting heavier loads with it. Anyway, this dude was called BOMB for Big Open Mouth Breather. Pretty apropos, says I.

SODA: Simply put, SODA stands for Shitty Officer, Disappoints All. He was just not the most reliable guy on the planet, and he had a very noncaring attitude about everything. He had zero sense of urgency when executing assigned tasks or whenever he was asked to do something by a friend. Some would say he had a high drift factor. The story given in evidence of his personal attributes was that he and a couple of other squadron pilots were getting ready to fly from Okinawa to San Diego for TAD (temporary additional duty). All were told to be ready at 0900 to load the van and head to the Naha International Airport. SODA set his alarm for 0900. When they knocked on his door to find out why he wasn't ready, he answered his door wearing only his boxers. In his arms was a bundle of dirty laundry. He just shrugged and said, "I'm gonna do some laundry real quick and then I'll be ready." He didn't take responsibility for making everyone late, and he was defensive about his need

to do laundry "real quick." They were supposed to be at the airport at 1000, and it was a forty-five-minute drive. Spoiler alert! They missed their flight.

⬥⬤⬥ THERE I WAS, INVERTED OVER THE RICE PADDIES . . .

Long ago when Afghanistan was still "winnable," I was working with some British forces in Helmand Province while the Brits conducted an IED-clearing operation through Gereshk along the Helmand River. I was at the Tactical Operations Center atop an old Russian base called Artillery Hill, and it was my job to coordinate fires (air and ground) for the patrols providing security for the explosives-clearing team. One of my teams came under fire and requested air support. The only thing I had available was an EA-6B Prowler doing silly circles in the sky at about 16,000 feet. The EA-6B does all kinds of supersecret-squirrel electronics stuff, but they don't usually carry air-to-ground ordnance. At the time, the Prowler crew were trying to pick up Taliban communications and locate their positions. I had no assets to provide that could actually drop warheads on foreheads, and at the time the Direct Air Support Center had no aircraft to give. I used my radio and asked the pilot of the Prowler if he could do a show of force to scare the Taliban away. I have never heard anyone so excited to do a show of force as the pilot of this EA-6B was when he responded in the affirmative. A show of force is just a low flyby over the enemy to scare them into breaking contact with friendly forces. The Prowler guys were used to the same-thing-different-day routine of flying in an orbit around a designated area for hours on end. Jet flying it may be, but I'm told it gets pretty boring up there. This pilot was more excited than Jeffrey Epstein at an all-girl's high school swim party. So down they came, screaming at 100 feet above ground level over the enemy's position, launching a torrent of blinding countermeasure flares as they flew past, terrifying everyone within a 15-mile radius with the sound of their engines. The EA-6B has the loudest jet noise known to man, which was useful because the Taliban ran away and didn't poke their heads up for the rest of the operation. I think I made that Prowler crew's day.

BIFF: Sounds like a pretty manly name, but not so much. This call sign was earned while the bearer was still in flight school. He was a big, buff dude who was nice to everyone; it was just his nature. However, he was overly nice to all the instructor pilots. His friends took notice. He was sucking up to get high scores on flights, the highest being five. "Hey sir, do you need anything? Can I get you a cup of coffee? I warmed your seat for you, sir." That kind of thing. BIFF stands for Blows Instructors for Fives. It may or may not have worked, because he did get jets out of primary and went on to be a Harrier pilot. The call sign he hated so much followed him to the fleet, much to his everlasting chagrin.

FAB: There was a CH-46 pilot who smelled terrible all the time! Take a bath, man! They said he smelled like Feet, Ass, and Balls. He claimed FAB was short for fabulous.

PUMBA: There was a weird fetish in a Marine Harrier squadron, wherein there had to be at least one pilot with a *Lion King*–related call sign. When that pilot departed, they would bestow one of the new guys with a call sign that was related to *The Lion King*. It's a tradition that stretches back to World War II . . . right. One of the pilots was a little bit pudgy and had what are commonly referred to in the pejorative as man boobs, or simply moobs. The geniuses in his squadron came up with PUMBA for Put Ur Man Boobs Away. Pretty good for an acronym call sign. Pretty good. Don't trouble yourself with the creative misspelling of the word "your." Just go with it.

DANGER

EJECTION
SEAT

DANGER

DANGER

MYSTERY

SAS makes sure he remembered his box nasty before his flight back to home station in Iwakuni, Japan.

WARNING - DO NOT CUT CANOPY
WITHIN 3 INCHES OF CANOPY FRAME

Cigar night on Pancho's Patio on board USS America

BC: There was a Navy pilot who had a massive cowlick on his head, and he always had his hair cut in such a way so as to reduce it. The way he wore his hair, which was a little longer than it should have been, resembled a butt crack. So, his call sign was Butt Cut.

NFOV: The targeting and image sensors that exist on modern combat aircraft would astound the lay person. F-18s for instance use forward-looking infrared (FLIR) to track targets, and there are four modes that they can use for better targeting data. Two modes are wide field of view (zoomed out) and narrow field of view (zoomed in). NFOV is the acronym used for narrow field of view. In a bar in Tokyo, I asked an F-18 pilot what his call sign was. He responded with NFOV. No explanation was necessary. I instantly understood why he had received this particular call sign. His eyes were freakishly close together.

CRAMR (like Kramer from *Seinfeld*): There are various versions of this call sign. When I wrote this I was on USS *Wasp* off the coast of Brisbane, Australia. The mentally challenged MH-60S pilot in question was in limbo as his squadron mates deliberated on his fate. In the balance was the call sign he would have for the rest of his life. CRAMR stands for Can't Read and Mentally Retarded. Another version is CRAMER, for Can't Read and May Eat Ritalin. Previously, this daredevil of the sky was given the temporary call sign of FIT, which stood for Functionally Illiterate Tony, but the guys in his squadron felt it didn't quite capture all that was Tony. Tony had trouble reading out loud, and some thought he may actually have slipped past the Navy's standards and gotten in without ever having learned to read. He's also tall, with a shock of black hair and an annoying habit of entering staterooms just like Kramer from *Seinfeld* to tell someone something that can't wait until the sun comes up, or while someone is in their room having a little "me time." So the combination of his likeness to Kramer from *Seinfeld* and the acronym of his mental acuity (or lack thereof) really comes together in this mix-and-match call sign. I hope his squadron mates went with CRAMR.

Tassels: You know how old-timey burlesque girls used to wear nipple tassels? That's kind of what this CH-46 pilot's call sign is named after. This poor guy went swimming with his squadron in Thailand, and it was discovered that he had unusually long nipple hair, as if he had hairy tassels.

AP/CAP: If you're a bit hard to get along with, your call sign will likely allude to something akin to A-hole or Douche Knob, something friendly you can tell your grandma about. There was this Cobra guy who just didn't get along with the instructor pilots at the RAG, so they started calling him A-hole Pilot or AP for short. I don't know why, or how, really. There must have been plenty of options, but for some reason AP was what they came up with. Needless to say, AP did not appreciate his call sign. When he showed up to his fleet squadron, he immediately started campaigning to have it changed. This is usually frowned upon in the pilot community, and unfortunately he had entered the most uncompromising and ruthless community known to humankind. The Cobra community tends to eat their young. Straight up, Cobra pilots are known for being assholes. His complaints fell on deaf ears, and his efforts only served to have the opposite effect. The more he campaigned, the more the call sign stuck. At the squadron kangaroo court a year after he had labored under the burden of his unwanted call sign, the CO announced that he would entertain changing AP's call sign. By this time AP had served in Afghanistan and had laid down some warheads on foreheads. As such, the CO felt that a call sign change was appropriate. The squadron pilots tried to shout down the CO's allowance of a call sign change with angry outbursts of dissent, but the CO used his authority to quell the rebellion. He said, "Look, AP has been to Afghanistan and he is a combat-tested pilot." AP's eyes lit

Sunset on command at sea. The CO of USS *Wasp* takes a last long walk on the flight deck with his command master chief and his XO. The next morning, the CO turned command over to his XO, and it would be the last time this CO would command at sea.

up. He felt that his campaigning was finally going to bring about a monumental change in his life. "Therefore," continued the CO, "AP shall from henceforth and in the presence of this august body of death cheaters be known as Combat Asshole Pilot." That probably wasn't the call sign CAP was hoping for.

OSLO: The C-130 pilot who earned this call sign may have been the inspiration for the United States Space Force. She was a bit of a space cadet without a space academy. Her head wasn't in the clouds, it was in outer space. As a result, she was given the collateral duty of Outer Space Liaison Officer.

Butters: There's a character on the popular TV cartoon series *South Park* who happens to perfectly personify in cartoon form an MH-60R pilot who was serving as the safety officer on USS *America* when I was there. Our Butters had a very self-deprecating sense of humor and was the ultimate "safety guy." As such, he could be a real buzzkill. His call sign isn't that funny if I can't show you a photo of him to show you exactly how much he actually resembled "Butters" from *South Park*, but the words of wisdom that would fall from his mouth, usually as non sequiturs, could make someone nearly blow their milk out their nose. Here's a couple of examples:

- "I have a tendency to be lame and safe. A lame duck is a safe duck."
- "Since coronavirus, sailors wearing their boots in the rack hasn't gone down even 1 percent."
- "I'm excited to get more RASberries on RAS day. Get it?"
- "Something I always wished about myself was that I was good at something."
- "I don't like beef. I like turkey burgers."

ATIS: In the world of aviation, most airfields have a frequency with an automated message that plays on a loop called ATIS. ATIS stands for Automated Terminal Information System. ATIS provides information for altimeter setting, current weather, runway information, etc., and the information is updated every hour or so. There was an MH-60S pilot who never stopped talking. You couldn't get a word in. He's probably talking right now. So, he was talking but no one was responding, like ATIS. I think this call sign may be overly flattering. I get it, the dude talks so much that everyone else is forced to listen without responding, but at least the Automated Terminal Information System shares useful information.

COWboy: There was a young captain in a Marine AV-8B squadron who was responsible for a lot of little crappy jobs as collateral to his main duties (if you think his main duties would be flying, you obviously have never been a naval aviator). These duties often included planning family fun days and squadron events for spouses. He worked very closely with the squadron CO's wife, who essentially bossed him around like he was her assistant. COWboy: CO's Wife's boy.

MUNG: This call sign story is long and distinguished ("Yeah, like my Johnson"). It really involves three call signs and sort of tracks the progress of a single AV-8B Harrier pilot's flying career. His first call sign was earned due to his being kind of a weird dude. He had been a goth in high school and college and hadn't completely given up that lifestyle. CAF stood for Creepy as F**k. One day while conducting his very first landing on a ship in the Harrier, his descent to the flight deck was a little too aggressive. The LSO called for power. Somehow the laws of physics were not working for CAF that day. When he applied power to slow his descent, it caused the jet to spin rapidly to the left and scrape the left wing across the flight deck. The LSO in the tower was screaming "EJECT, EJECT, EJECT" on the radio, but CAF stuck with it and somehow managed to gain altitude and fly away to fly another day. There were

At the end of a flight in his F-35B, SHOCK unstraps from his ejection seat.

An LSE stands with her back to the wake of the mighty USS *Wasp* somewhere on the South China Sea.

other incidents that almost cost him his life, and his squadron mates began to believe that the Harrier gods were trying to kill him. For his multiple brushes with death, he earned the call sign Cat, because he seemed to have nine lives. Through all of this, he was still creepy. One day he got caught cheating on his annual closed-book NATOPS test—he had the NATOPS open in his lap—which earned him the call sign MUNG for May Use NATOPS for Guidance. The *Urban Dictionary* defines a Mung as a person who sneaks into cemeteries at night, exhumes bodies from fresh graves, and, while standing on the gravestone, leaps in the air like a wrestler from the corner of a wrestling ring and body-slams the cadaver in order to make all of the internal gases and juices burst forth in a disgusting display of gross. The acronym was completely made up simply so MUNG's squadron mates would have an excuse to call their creepy AF, nine-lives-having, closed-book-test-cheating, fellow Harrier pilot a name associated with one of the creepiest acts known to man.

SPECIAL THANKS

This book is dedicated to the rare breed of human being who pines to fly in the naval services around the world, and the even-rarer breed who earns the wings of gold of a US naval aviator or NFO. I would also like to give a shout-out to the following individuals: PAM, Cherub, Flanders, Pocket, Scally, Donny, Bobby, Pancho, G-Roy, SAS, Dickens, Elton, BT, Machine, GUTTS, Big Bird, Mush, Alpha, Marbles, Nibbles (Astro), Dick, Waldo, Asphalt, Brazzers, Tosser, Koncha, Climax, Scooby, Smash, Stroke, Salsa, the Dragons, the Flying Tigers, the Boonie Sharks, "The Knightriders," the Archangel OGs, the Green Knights, the Flying Leathernecks, the USS *Wasp* and USS *America* wardrooms, and every other salty dawg who shared a call sign story with me. A special thanks goes out to Birdbath for providing the most epic call sign story ever. And to Aunt Barb for a solid sanity check and the kind of encouragement only an aunt can provide.

SPECIAL THANKS

Two sailors dressed in their whites pull down the ship's ensign at sunset in Okinawa, Japan.

Sometimes even the ships get unflattering call signs . . . unofficial, of course.

USS *Essex* [LHD-2]: "The E-sucks," also "the Big Gray Deuce," "Steamin' Deuce," and "Stressex"

USS *Kittyhawk*: "The Shitty Kitty"

USS *Wasp*: "We Ain't Seeing Ports" because it rarely pulled in anywhere when it was underway. It was also called "Building One" because it spent so much time in the yards.

USS *Saipan* [LHA-2]: "The Big Deuce" (when the ship went underway, the crew would snicker that "the Deuce is loose!")

USS *Kearsarge*: "The Beer Barge"

USS *Abraham Lincoln*: "Babe Lincoln," because in 1995 it was the first aircraft carrier to deploy with women on board. Also, "Stinkin' Lincoln."

USS *Oriskany*: "The Big Risk"

USS *Carl Vinson*: "Chuck Bucket"

USS *Enterprise*: "Enterprison." Apparently, they didn't see a lot of liberty ports.

USS *Forrestal*: "Firestal," so named after the fire aboard that nearly destroyed the ship in 1967; also "Zippo."

USS *Bonhomme Richard* [LHD-6]: "Motel 6," because it spent so much time in the yard it was more of a building than an actual warship. Also "Bonnie Dick."

USS *Bataan* [LHD-5]: "The Dirty Nickel," or "Cell Block 5"

APPENDIX

air boss: A seasoned naval aviator who is the god of all flight deck and flight operations that occur in the immediate vicinity of the carrier. The air boss's word is law, and failure to adhere to the air boss's authority will lead to a swift and sharp reprimand over the loudspeakers for all present to witness. The air boss works in the tower, calls the shots, executes the air plan, and takes zero crap from anyone. Do not cross the air boss.

attaboy: The second-highest praise a naval aviator can receive from the air boss

bandit: Code word for enemy aircraft, not to be confused with bogie

behind the power curve: You never want to fall behind the power curve while flying. This is especially true while landing. If your aircraft is creating more drag than your engines can quickly overcome, you may find yourself in a little bit of a pickle. Usually, a pilot finds themselves behind the power curve due to a temporary loss of situational awareness. Outside the cockpit, anyone who is behind the power curve, either momentarily or permanently, is a person who has lost situational awareness.

Big Blue Sleeping Pill: The NATOPS is not a riveting read. It's written by the same people who write the assembly instructions for IKEA furniture. Imagine being compelled to read hundreds of pages of IKEA assembly instructions out of professional requirement and as a matter of life and death. Also, imagine if you had to memorize many of the assembly instructions verbatim, which meant that not only did you have to read the many assembly instructions, but that you had to go over them again and again until by rote they were implanted in your brain. The cover of the NATOPS is blue. You get it.

Bingo: Refers to the reading on your fuel gauge that tells you it's a good idea to return to base and land or else risk running out of gas before you're able to do so. This is based on the distance you have to fly to return to the ship or base. NATOPS requires that pilots must land with a certain amount of fuel in their fuel tanks. This amount varies per aircraft but is generally referred to as NATOPS mins (minimums). In a bar you could use this term to indicate you're almost out of money and it's time to go.

boat: A boat is something you take out into the middle of a lake and fish from. It has oars and little benches to sit on while you cast your line in to catch some trout. But we in naval aviation refer to the mighty ship we fly from simply as "the boat." SWOs don't like it when we do that, and they are quick to remind us that the boat is a mighty US naval warship. Yeah, whatever SHOE.

bogie: Code word for an unidentified aircraft, with the potential of being a foe. Once a bogie is confirmed to be a bad guy, it becomes a bandit.

bought the farm: Back in the old days, when all military airfields were surrounded by miles and miles of farmland, every time a plane crashed in a farmer's field, the farmer could sue the government for the damage to his crops. Back then, aviation was not just unforgiving, but it was inherently dangerous. Many aviators paid the ultimate price in pursuit of the dream to soar with the eagles. If you crashed and died, the money paid out to the farmer was enough to buy his farm, and therefore, by crashing, the aviator had "bought the farm."

Bravo Zulu: Bravo, well done!

bubba: This is a term to describe other kinds of pilots and NFOs. For instance, CH-53E pilots are shitter bubbas. F-18 pilots are jet bubbas, etc., etc., etc.

buster: Go as fast as possible, or hurry the hell up!

Charlie pattern: landing pattern around a ship.

clearing turn: When you fly helicopters, it's a good idea to occasionally maneuver your aircraft around to see what other aircraft may be in your general vicinity. But there is another way to use this flight safety term. When you're in squadron spaces, and you want to talk trash about the CO, it's a good idea to do a "clearing turn" with your head to make sure the CO or their lackey is not in earshot.

Code Brown: Navy H-60 pilot slang for the need to land immediately so someone can vacate their bowels

CAVU: Ceiling and visibility unrestricted, also severe clear; counter term for severe thunderstorms or severe weather

Charlie Foxtrot: Cluster f**k. A cluster f**k is so bad that it resembles a cluster bomb. When a cluster bomb reaches a certain height aboveground after being dropped, it releases hundreds of little bomblets, which can really make a mess of things. Additionally, not all the little bomblets explode, so the area where the cluster bomb was dropped becomes a minefield. So a cluster f**k is like a cluster bomb. It's just a term for a really bad situation or when nothing goes to plan and the mission goes off the rails. It can also be used to describe a person, as in "You are a walking cluster f**k."

check six: Aviators use a clock code system when directing other aviators within their aircraft or their flight to a bogie or point of interest. Twelve o'clock equates to the nose of the aircraft and six o'clock equates to the tail of the aircraft. In dogfighting, you don't want to end up with a bandit on your six o'clock position, so fighter pilots are constantly checking their "six." Saying "check six" is also slang for telling someone to watch what they're saying around certain individuals, or to watch your back.

combat dump: Taking a last-minute crap before a mission

dash-two: The second aircraft in a formation flight. The lead aircraft is never referred to as dash-one. Rather, the lead aircraft is always referred to as "lead."

deck hit: Pilot slang for landing on a flight deck for fuel, passengers, mail, or cargo before taking off again and continuing on mission

Delta Sierra: Dumb shit

double nuts: Any aircraft with 00 for a side number. Usually the CO's bird.

drift factor: An aviator who has a high drift factor is considered unreliable.

the **drink**: This is a term for the ocean. A person who ends up in the ocean by either crashing their aircraft or falling off the ship is in the drink. You don't want to be in the drink.

feet wet/dry: Naval terminology for flying over the boundary between water (wet) and land (dry). For instance, if someone flew over the beach on their way out to sea, they would report that they were "feet wet." If crossing the beach on the way to a land-based target, they would say, "Feet dry."

FOD: Foreign-object debris. Bits and pieces that end up on flight decks that can get sucked into an engine, causing damage and risking lives.

fun meter pegged: Cockpit instrumentation has meters with needles that indicate the scale of operational limitation for engines, vertical speed, oil pressure, etc. It is never a good thing if one of these meters is pegged all the way to the left or right, because it usually indicates that the device for which the meter is used is either not working or is operating beyond acceptable limitations (it could also mean that the gauge is just broken). When someone's fun meter is pegged, it means they aren't having a good time.

FRS: After a naval aviator first comes out of flight school, they are usually sent to SERE (Survive, Evade, Resist, and Escape) school, followed immediately by a stop at the FRS before checking in to their first fleet squadron. FRS stands for fleet replacement squadron, and each aircraft platform has one. For instance, F-18 pilots check in to VFA-106 or VMFAT-101 to learn how to fly the F-18. The military is constantly renaming organizations because new commanders really want to put their name on a place, and they do so by going for low-hanging fruit when looking for something to change. The acronym associated with the organization is usually the easiest target. The FRS used to be called the RAG (rag), which stood for replacement air group. The term "RAG" was around for so long that even to this day, even among pilots and NFOs who've only ever been to the FRS, the FRS is still called the RAG. Calling it the RAG gives it that air of old school. I attended the CH-46E FRS, but the change from RAG to FRS had only just occurred. When I checked in to my first squadron, some of the older pilots still referred to the RAG, and in order to fit in, younger guys like me did likewise. So when I became one of the old hands in the squadron, along with others, and all of us were still using the term "RAG" instead of FRS, the younger guys also called it the RAG. It will take a very long time until FRS fully replaces RAG in the lexicon of naval aviation. In this book, RAG and FRS are interchangeable.

Gs: A single G is 14.7 pounds per square inch, which is what you are experiencing as you read this. Aircraft tend to produce forces during turns and climbs that increase the G loading. So if you are in a 6 G turn, you will experience six times your own body weight.

GAF: Give a f**k, as in "I don't have one to give." Example: He GAFed off his responsibilities.

goo: Bad weather that makes it impossible to see (i.e., in the clouds). Also "in the soup."

gouge: The latest inside information. It also refers to study guides in flight school created by student naval aviators to share with SNAs further behind in the curriculum. Gouge is not always up to date or accurate. Student naval aviators who tend to rely on the gouge, instead of digging into the books, risk falling prey to the following flight school axiom: Live by the gouge, die by the gouge.

Hail and Bail: Squadrons and wardrooms have a party every two or three months to welcome new people and say goodbye to people who are leaving. Other naval commands do this as well. The official term for this party is Hail and Farewell, which is a naval tradition that stretches back centuries. Hail and Bail, which rhymes, is the flippant version for yet another mandatory fun event that no one really wants to go to.

head: Back in the old days of wooden ships with sails, sailors relieved themselves at the bow of the ship. Oftentimes, the bow was referred to as the head, so if a sailor had to "soft duck" some SEALs, they did so at the head. For the sake of tradition, bathrooms on ships to this day are referred to as "heads." Sailors and marines will often state that they are going to "hit the head," but they don't mean they are going to go hit their head against something. It just means that they are going to the bathroom to drop some kids off at the pool.

head on a swivel: Term used for maintaining situational awareness. A person with their head on a swivel is always looking around, spotting the potential dangers and hazards around them. Often used in combat among pilots and among carrier flight deck crews who risk walking into intakes, jet exhausts, and spinning propeller blades if they lose situational awareness.

IFR: Instrument flight rules. When the weather is bad and the pilot must rely on their cockpit instruments to fly and navigate.

IFR: I follow roads. Also applies to the above IFR definition. For helicopter pilots, if the weather brings the ceilings low enough, they can sometimes fly lower to stay out of the clouds. If a road can help a driver navigate to their destination, why not a helicopter pilot?

Iron Tadpole: Nickname for the EA-6B Prowler because of its bulbous nose and pointy tail

JOPA: Junior Officer Protection Agency. There is a saying often shared among lieutenants and captains that goes, "Die like a hero or live long enough to become the villain." What this means is that you either do something so stupid in your JO career that it permanently destroys any hope of promotion to major or lieutenant commander, or you jump through the career wickets and eventually become one of the lobotomy recipients known as field-grade officers. Field-grade officers cannot be trusted, and therefore there must be an organization willing to protect the JO community from the stupidity and treachery of field-grade officers.

kick the tires and light the fires: A term for conducting a quicker-than-normal preflight before launching. This term was made popular by Harry Connick Jr. in the film *Independence Day*. Connick played a Marine F-18 pilot in the film and said this phrase at the conclusion of the prebattle flight brief.

leap-ex: When something seemingly unimportant has to be done immediately in order to please the brass. One must leap through fiery hoops for reasons that defy logic. Ex is short for exercise.

liberty: When a ship pulls into port, the sailors are granted liberty at the discretion of the captain to go ashore and enjoy the delights and attractions offered in a new and exotic location. A lot of call signs are earned while marines and sailors are on liberty. It's an old mariners' term that goes back centuries, and I can honestly say with complete sincerity that there is nothing better than being a marine or sailor on liberty in some exotic port that most Americans have never heard of.

liberty boat: Aircraft carriers rarely tie up at a pier when they visit foreign ports. Most often they anchor offshore, and they use small ships to transport thirsty sailors and marines to a pier. Each boat holds roughly 30–40 people, so the wait to get ashore for a ship with roughly 6,000 people on board can be a little long. The worst part is coming back to the ship after a night of drinking. Most people are a bit drunk, and the bobbing of the boat in rough seas late at night can be terrible on the sensitive stomachs of drunk marines and sailors.

libo risk: There's always that one guy. You just know that if there is one person in the squadron who is going to screw it up for everyone while on liberty, it's this one guy or gal. They drink too much, they start fights, they have no control over their sexual appetites, and they have been known to return from liberty after liberty has expired. Maybe you're the liberty risk. Beware the liberty risk. These dudes ruin libo for everyone else. It takes only one.

LSO: Landing signals officer. Squadron pilot with a lot of experience in operating on and off naval shipping. LSOs assist flying pilots with landings and score their landing performance.

mandatory fun: A squadron party that you don't have to go to, but you are "highly encouraged" to attend. Also called "mando fun."

Martin Baker fan club: Refers to the rare group of aviators who have ejected from an aircraft and lived to tell the tale in a Martin Baker ejection seat. Martin Baker is a British company that produces the finest ejection seats the world over. When you enter this exclusive club, you'll receive a necktie from Martin Baker, with the company logo embroidered on it in a striped pattern. You are also eligible to purchase a limited-edition Martin Baker Breitling wristwatch that can be sold only to aircrew who have ejected from a doomed aircraft in a Martin Baker ejection seat.

mini boss: The assistant air boss on a carrier

mother/mom: The ship from which you launched and you will return to after you complete your mission

naval aviation planning: code for sneaking off to a stateroom for a nap. "I'm going to go and do some naval aviation planning." When I was on USS *America*, the guy who wrote the "plan of the day" (POD) was tricked into adding naval aviation planning from 1300 to 1500 on the schedule for an entire week before the XO, a naval aviator who was in the know, finally decided NAP time should be removed from the POD.

no joy: Failure to visually acquire a target or other aircraft, or failure to establish radio communications. "You followed Cmdr. Heatherly below (the hard deck) after he lost sight of you and called 'no joy.' Why?"

nugget: New pilot just checking in to his first squadron or a pilot who has never landed on a ship other than at flight school. First-tour new guy.

Phrog: The best nickname ever given to an aircraft in the naval services. The CH-46 looks like a smiling frog from the front. The stub wings look like a frog's legs, ready to leap at a moment's notice, and the chin bubble windows are shaped in an unmistakable smile. The CH-46 is a happy little helicopter! What's murky about this happy little helicopter's name is the spelling of frog with Ph instead of F. Whatever the reason, Marine CH-46 pilots have been calling it the Phrog since the Vietnam War, and whenever there is another f-word associated with the word Phrog, it too is spelled with the famous Ph (e.g., "Phrogs Phorever!").

pickle: To purposely drop a bomb, external fuel tank, or underslung load. Sometimes used as slang for going number two.

pinkie time: Landings that occur after sunset, but before the end of twilight. Technically, any landing after sunset is considered a night landing for the purposes of currency and proficiency, especially in the Navy where there is no distinction between high-light-level night landings and low-light-level night landings. The Marine Corps holds itself to this unnecessary standard, which really only serves to frustrate operations officers and pilot-training officers in their tireless efforts to keep everyone current and proficient. In the Navy, JOs sneeringly refer to "pinkie time" as the "field-grade officers night-flying hour."

playmates: Not Playboy bunnies. Other pilots in other aircraft who are on the same mission or in the same squadron as you.

plopter: Derisive term for the MV-22B, because it doesn't really land, it just sort of plops into places. Since it does so vertically the way a helicopter does, it's a plopter. Also, plopter is the words "plane" and "helicopter" mashed together.

poopy suit: It gets cold out over the ocean blue sometimes. When you fly from Navy ships, there's always a small chance that you may have to bail out or ditch, and if you do so, your poopy suit will protect you from hypothermia after long periods floating in frigid water. A poopy suit is simply an extra layer of waterproof flight gear that is meant to preserve your body temperature in the unfortunate event you have to spend a considerable time waiting in icy waters for a helicopter to come and rescue your unlucky butt. It's referred to as a poopy suit because once it's on, it's not exactly easy to get off. This means you're more likely to soil yourself in a poopy suit than if you were just wearing a flight suit. At least in a flight suit, you can easily wriggle your way out of it if nature calls. Not so in a poopy suit.

preflighting: While not grammatically correct, this is an actual verb used by pilots and aircrew throughout naval aviation. Before each flight, pilots and aircrew visually inspect the aircraft by conducting a walk-around, shaking various parts to ensure they are properly attached, checking fluids, and other various visual inspections to ensure that the aircraft isn't going to come apart in flight or run out of hydraulic fluid and kill everyone on board. There is another use of the term "preflighting" that has nothing to do with aircraft. Before going out for a night on the town, aviators will gather at someone's house and have a couple of drinks to get into the spirit of things. It's called preflighting because it's what you do before you take a flight on the magical airplane called alcohol.

pucker factor: The human body gives several physical indications of terror when a person gets scared. One such indication is that the anus shrinks in size, as if it puckers like your lips do when you kiss someone on the cheek. When your ass puckers, it's because you are pretty sure you're about to die. Pucker factor is an imaginary measurement of how scared you were in any given scenario. In other words, how puckered was your ass when you had a near-miss collision with your wingman? I've heard of some guys who achieved such a high pucker factor that they had to pull their seat cushions out of their butt cracks.

pulling chocks: When an aircraft is ready to depart the line and either taxi to the runway or lift from the ship, the pilot gives the "pull chocks" hand and arm signal. Imagine two thumbs up and the bottom of the hands touching each other with the thumbs sticking out. The pilot moves their hands outward and back again, bumping the palms together to indicate that they are ready to have the chocks pulled out from the wheels so they can taxi or lift. But the "pull chocks" signal is also used by naval aviators and NFOs to tell their fellow naval aviators and NFOs that it's time to leave, whether it be a bar, a meal, or a sticky situation on liberty in Thailand or the Philippines. They can either say, "Let's pull chocks" or simply give the signal described above from across a crowded room. Pilots' and NFOs' spouses and children are often familiar with this useful hand and arm signal as well.

punch out: Slang for ejecting from a doomed aircraft or leaving an undesirable location such as a lame mandatory fun party at the CO's house

R2D2: Derogatory term for NFOs who occupy the seat behind the pilot, as R2D2 did behind Luke Skywalker on the X-wing

roger wilco: When a student naval aviator first begins flight school, they go through a course called API in Pensacola, Florida. API stands for Aviation Preparation Indoctrination. The SNAs learn everything they ever wanted to know about weather, engines, aerodynamics, and other flight-related subjects they will need to have a basic understanding of before they first fly in a training aircraft with an instructor pilot. The most important thing drilled into their heads, other than how to properly fall, is that they shall never utter the phrase "roger wilco!" "Roger" means that you understand. "Wilco" is short for "will comply." If you say the word "wilco," it's assumed that you understand, and therefore "roger" is extraneous and unnecessary. And if you go to the fleet and let slip "roger wilco" from your baby-like lips over the radio, you're gonna get an earful from the senior pilots, who detest that most hated rookie phrase. But, if you're a smart-ass, and you really just want to piss off someone who is a little too wrapped around the axle, by all means shout, "roger wilco" to the heavens!

SAS3: The MH-60 Seahawk helicopter has a system that helps the pilot better control the aircraft by dampening input controls and increasing stability. It's called the Stability Augmentation System (SAS). There are two such systems on the 60, SAS1 and SAS2. There is no SAS3. However, if you're new and aren't very good, or you suck at flying in general, the HAC will sometimes "ride" the controls with you and make minor inputs to make sure that you don't kill everyone on board by crashing. When a HAC does this he's activated the "SAS3." Get it? Afterward, instructor pilots might joke among themselves that the last copilot needed a lot of SAS3. Ego can also play a factor. When two peers fly together and one decides the other needs a little SAS3, whether deserved or not, the pilot on the controls will sneeringly tell the other pilot to turn off the SAS3.

section: Two aircraft operating in a single flight, with a designated flight leader and a dash-two

severe clear: When it comes to weather, the prefix "severe" usually indicates the kind of weather no one wants to fly in. However, when the weather is CAVU, some pilots will refer to the weather as severe clear, meaning that the skies are so beautiful, the only word to adequately describe them in prefix form is "severe."

SHOE: Derogatory term for surface warfare officers who wear black shoes, as opposed to the more stylish brown shoes worn by Navy air wing officers and chief petty officers. SHOE is also an acronym for "stupidest humans on earth."

skids: Refers to the UH-1 and AH-1. Plenty of helicopters around the world have skid-like landing gear, but in the Marines the only helicopters to have skids are UH-1 Hueys and AH-1 Cobras.

skid kids: Derisive term for the pilots who fly UH-1 Hueys and AH-1 Cobras

skipper: CO of a squadron or a naval aviator who becomes captain of a ship

shit hot: Also, Sierra Hotel. The highest praise you can receive from a naval aviator.

shitter: Slang for a CH-53E or MH-53. They are so called because when they fly, black exhaust pours out of the engines and gets blown in a downward trajectory by the rotor wash. 53s poo all over the sky.

soft duck: Helicopter pilot slang for taking a dump. Officially, it's a term used to describe the insertion of recon or SEALs by pushing a rubber boat off the helicopter's ramp into the water, followed closely behind by the men who do the snooping and pooping (that's just a euphemism for spec ops stuff). The helicopter enters a 10-foot hover taxi over the water to accomplish this, and when a helicopter does a soft duck, it looks like it's taking a giant crap.

stub wing check: Phrog pilot slang for urinating. On most Navy and Marine Corps helicopters, there are little stub wings that stick out from the fuselage. These stub wings contain fuel cells and are mounting points for the main landing gear. The best place to urinate under the CH-46 with rotors spinning while on the ground is the point on the front of the stub wing where it is connected to the fuselage. Just press your body into the corner and let loose. This usually results in a mess-free pee, because under the aircraft is a dead spot for the rotor wash coming from the spinning blades. When this doesn't work is when the smart-ass pilot still holding the flight controls pulls in just a tiny bit of collective so the rotor wash reaches under the aircraft and sprays your stream onto the legs of your flight suit.

three down and locked: Confirmation a pilot gives to the air boss or air control tower that their landing gear is extended and locked in place prior to landing. An even-slangier term is "three in the breeze." My last radio call on my last flight in Iraq was "Tiki Tower, Islander 64 is three in the breeze, over the trees, full stop–last stop, short final for the Rock!" The original phrase for "three in the breeze, over the trees" came from the old days of flight training in Pensacola. At Saufley Airfield near Pensacola there was a copse of trees used as a reporting point for student naval aviators. When they flew over that particular cluster of trees, they indicated that they were "over the trees, with three down and locked." Some clever git came up with "three in the breeze, over the trees," and it sort of stuck for a while, until the course rules changed and the fancy rhyme faded away into memory. I heard the story from an old Marine pilot who remembered the good old days. By the way, the "Tiki Tower" was a reference to the air control tower at Al Toqaddum Airbase in Anbar Province, Iraq. Pilots just called it "TQ tower" because it was easier to say than Al Toqaddum. If you said TQ fast enough, it just sounded like Tiki, so that's what some guys called it. "The Rock" was the ramp my squadron flew in and out of. We named it after the nickname that marines had given Okinawa, Japan, which is where my squadron was from, and since we were from an island, we chose "Islander" to be our squadron call sign. In case you were wondering, there were no trees.

warm fuzzy: You know that feeling you get when all is well, the bad man is gone, and you're home safe with Mommy? That's a warm fuzzy. Somehow this is slang in naval aviation for all is good to go. An example would be to make sure the skipper has a warm fuzzy about the cross-country flight to Las Vegas, so he'll sign off on it.

wingman: You all know this term. We use it the same way you do. You go to a bar, and your wingman is there to help you pick up that one member of the opposite sex you have your eye on. The origin of the term came from military aviation. While flying, your wingman is your dash-two, the pilot who flies on your wing when you fly as a section. Your wingman always has your six! It's a sex-neutral term. Wingperson doesn't quite work. Iceman: "You can be my wingman anytime." Maverick: "Bullshit, you can be mine!"

yanking and banking: Essentially, the pilot is yanking on the controls, banking the aircraft back and forth in order to navigate at low level through a canyon or to avoid enemy antiaircraft fire. Great balls of fire!

An Amtrack drops into the water off the coast of Okinawa off the welldeck ramp of the USS *Wasp*. The entire vehicle will submerge and then rise to the surface on its way to shore.

A tow crew pulls a folded up MV-22B to a spot in preparation for flight ops. It's not as easy as it looks.

A folded CH-53E in silhouette as the sun goes down over the South China Sea on board the USS *Wasp*.

you fail your SWO Board because
at to movie night instead
dying like the CO told you to.

Keep your tears in your eyes
where they belong.

HAT'S A CLEVER HIDING SPOT FOR
THE CEREAL YOU HAVE THERE...

BE A SHAME IF SOMEONE

DISCOVERED IT

BAY. WORST. LIBO. PORT. EVER!!!

NTERNET WILL HEAR OF THIS

BEER CALL

Australia

EXC
W

DR(

I WANT MAN
OVERBOARD
MUSTER
COMPLETED IN
LESS THAN 12
MINUTES!!!

XO

BE AFRAID!

UE FALCON

GOOD IDEA
FAIRY

DOUBLE
DRAGON

CHAIN
MONSTER

HEY'RE ON THE PROWL

SIR, I DON'T
MEAN TO BE A
BUZZ KILL, BUT
THESE DUDES
STILL NEED TO
DO THEIR ZONE
INSPECTIONS!

Types of Headaches

Migraine   Hypertension

BOS'N Mate's
Stress   Lunch Piping

AUG 12   AUG 13

...LACKLUSTER

YEEAAAAHM

US: YAY, PATROL 20.1 IS ALMOST OVER!

C7F:

ACKCHYUALLY

Bos'n Mate inhaling befo
last blow at "Lunch for th

USS ROOSEVELT

PILLS THAT MAKE
YOU STARE AT
GOOD IDEAS

THIS IS MY
LAST PATROL,
SO I DON'T
CARE
ANYMORE...

AIR OPS

...

I'M ONLY
JOKING. I
NEVER DID.

CALL

NYPD

WASP

CTF76